Culturally Responsive
Lessons & Activities

Grade 2

Writing: Monika Davies
　　　　　Leslie Barnard Booth
Content Editing: Teera Robinson
　　　　　Lisa Vitarisi Mathews
Copy Editing: Laurie Westrich
Art Direction: Yuki Meyer
Cover Design: Yuki Meyer
Illustration: Mary Rojas
Design/Production: Paula Acojido
　　　　　Yuki Meyer
　　　　　Jessica Onken

EMC 8262

Evan-Moor®

Visit
teaching-standards.com
to view a correlation
of this book.
This is a free service.

**Correlated to
Current Standards**

**Congratulations on your purchase of some of the
finest teaching materials in the world.**

*Photocopying the pages in this book
is permitted for <u>single-classroom use only</u>.
Making photocopies for additional classes
or schools is prohibited.*

For information about other Evan-Moor products, call 1-800-777-4362,
fax 1-800-777-4332, or visit our website, www.evan-moor.com.
Entire contents © 2022 Evan-Moor Corporation
18 Lower Ragsdale Drive, Monterey, CA 93940-5746. Printed in USA.

CPSIA: Bradford & Bigelow, Newburyport, MA USA　[12/2022]

Contents

8 Nonfiction, Informational Fiction, and Realistic Fiction Units

The units in this book are about people from diverse backgrounds, with different abilities, ethnicities, and origins. Four units feature nonfiction biographical stories or informational fiction stories about people who are inspirational and perseverant. Four units feature realistic fiction stories about authentic situations and challenges that real people experience. Each unit has a different theme and begins with a teacher page that introduces the subject and activities. The story pages and activities are reproducible for students. The unit's theme is shown at the top of each student page.

Examples of themes include:

Dreams Do Come True

Other People Can't Stop You

Learning Helps You Do Great Things

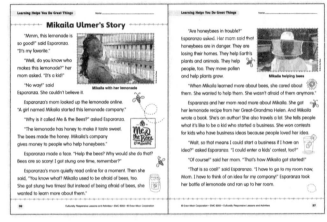

Story

Each of the nonfiction, informational fiction, and realistic fiction units has a reproducible two-page story that the subsequent activities relate to. The story emphasizes the unit's theme.

The stories describe real-life experiences in an age-appropriate way. They tell how people overcame challenges, navigated through complicated situations, and made choices that defined their lives. All of these story subjects and themes were chosen thoughtfully because of their power to inspire and the importance of representation.

Theme-Based Activities

Each unit has an activity that students complete independently, a whole-class or small-group discussion activity, a partner activity, and a project menu. Students choose from hands-on projects, performance projects, and creative writing projects.

Activities in all units vary and are designed to be engaging and open-ended, with a wide variety of response formats. The goal is for students to feel like the activities are providing a "safe space" to share their own unique viewpoints and experiences.

Activities include the following:

- creative writing and drawing
- critical thinking
- games
- visual information
- discussion
- hypothetical scenarios and problem solving
- making choices and justifying opinions
- art projects

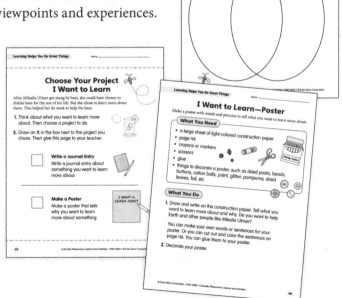

3 Cultural Exploration and Self-Discovery Units

The cultural exploration and self-discovery units are not centered around a text; rather, they feature a variety of engaging and creative activities that invite students to reflect on their own cultures and interactions with the world. The activities prompt students to share their own opinions, tastes, families, and experiences. These activities also support students in being culturally responsive by keeping an open mind, learning about the people around them with the intention of recognizing their value, and considering other viewpoints. Many of the activities provide opportunities for collaboration and whole-class projects. Some collaborative activities include making a class mural, writing a letter to a friend, and playing games.

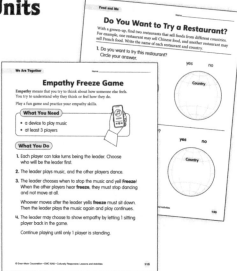

Student Resources

Additional pages provide students with support and provide opportunities for students to take an active role in their learning.

Student Contents

You may wish to allow your students to choose a unit to complete. Reproduce and distribute the Student Contents to students. Review the Student Contents with students. Read aloud the choices of units and descriptions. Have students think about what they are interested in reading, and let the class choose a unit.

How Do I Say It?

Reproduce and distribute the page to students. The text at the top of the page explains the purpose. This page models respectful language that kids may choose to use during a class or group discussion. Read aloud the text and sentences on the page as students follow along silently. Discuss with students what listening, showing respect, and being kind looks and sounds like. You may wish to distribute this page to students before you begin the first unit.

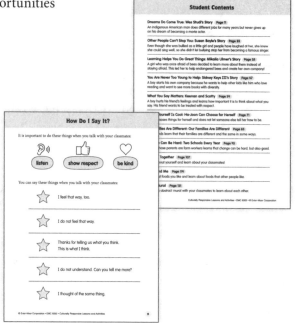

Student and Parent/Guardian Sharing Forms

The Student and Parent/Guardian Sharing Forms are intended to provide a connection between home and school. The purpose is to invite students and their families to communicate directly with the teacher and to take an active role in their learning.

How to Use This Book

Planning Instruction
Nonfiction, Informational Fiction, and Realistic Fiction Units

Teacher Pages

Each unit begins with a teacher page that summarizes the focus of the unit and provides a suggested teaching path.

Nonfiction, Informational Fiction, and Realistic Fiction Stories

These units center around the story and theme, such as Dreams Do Come True. The story provides context for the activities and projects. You can choose the activities that align with your students' needs or provide opportunities to increase engagement and positive interactions among students. Or you can allow students to choose the theme or person they would like to read about by reproducing the Student Contents on page 8 and distributing it to students.

Independent Activities

Each nonfiction, informational fiction, and realistic fiction story is followed by an independent activity that provides students opportunities to reflect on the story and the theme and relate it to their own lives.

Discussion Activities

Each unit includes a discussion activity. Before the discussion, students read the discussion items that are based on the story and theme. They are asked to think about their own opinions and experiences, and they may choose to write about them in preparation for the discussion. Before you begin the whole- and small-group discussions, you may wish to reproduce and distribute page 9, How Do I Say It? This page provides ideas and suggestions for statements and sentence starters that encourage respectful and productive communication.

Partner Activities

Each unit includes partner activities that are intended to help students learn about each other as they also learn more about themselves. To prepare for these activities, consider how you will assign partners or what process you will use to have students choose partners. It is important that students connect with classmates that they may not have in their social circle.

Choose Your Project Activities

Each unit includes a project menu for students to choose from. The project choices include hands-on, performance, and creative writing projects. Many of the projects require materials that are commonly part of classroom art supplies. Before you distribute the Choose Your Project activities to students, you may wish to confirm that you have access to the materials needed.

Cultural Exploration and Self-Discovery Units

Teacher Pages

Each unit begins with a teacher page that summarizes the focus of the unit and provides an overview of the activities and projects in the unit.

Activities, Games, and Projects

These units focus on learning about oneself and others through the lens of culture, family traditions, and people's similarities and differences. The activities, games, and projects range from individual to collaborative and often extend to home and family.

The pages in these units do not have to be completed in sequential order. Choose the activities that you want your students to complete, or offer them the opportunity to choose based on their interests.

About Culturally Responsive Teaching and Learning

Culturally responsive teaching is about connecting students' cultures and life experiences with what they are learning in school. Cultural responsiveness is creating a climate in which all students can feel a sense of belonging while also feeling safe to be their authentic selves as they process the curriculum and academic content.

These are some things you might see in a culturally responsive learning environment:

- Student-choice learning activities
- Students sharing about their home lives, first languages, or other cultural and personal experiences
- A sense of community as an emphasis during learning, in addition to academic content
- Family involvement in the learning process

Evan-Moor's Approach to Culturally Responsive Teaching and Learning

The activities in this book are designed to provide students with choices for how to demonstrate their learning and unique viewpoints. Many of the activities, including the group discussions, give students the opportunity to share about their own families and experiences. Our goal is to help students explore their own individualities, cultures, and life experiences and to help them learn more about their classmates, as well as to help teachers gain insights about who their students are so they can make every student's learning more meaningful. The authentic stories in this book represent people from many backgrounds and reflect the diversity and life experiences of people in our world. We hope these stories are both inspiring and enlightening for students.

Student Contents

Culturally Responsive Lessons and Activities • EMC 8262 • © Evan-Moor Corporation

How Do I Say It?

It is important to do these things when you talk with your classmates:

You can say these things when you talk with your classmates:

 I feel that way, too.

_____

 I do not feel that way.

_____

 Thanks for telling us what you think.
This is what I think.

_____

 I do not understand. Can you tell me more?

_____

 I thought of the same thing.

Student Sharing Form

Name _____

Answer the questions below or write to tell your teacher anything you want to share about.

Write about or draw something you want to tell the class about your family or your life.

```



```

Parent/Guardian Sharing Form

This is an optional form to help build a sense of community in our class.
Please contribute an idea if you wish to.

Name _____

Is there anything that you would like your child's classmates to learn about
that relates to your family's culture or your family's/your child's experiences?   **Yes   No**

If yes, please write to explain:

_____

_____

_____

_____

_____

Dreams Do Come True

Wes Studi's Story

This unit is about trying to do what you love to do. Even if you already have another job or think it's too late, it's never too late to do what you love. Students will read about Wes Studi, a Cherokee American actor, whose dreams came true. Students may already have their own dreams for the future and may be thinking about how to accomplish those dreams, so they may connect to Wes Studi's story, or they may learn how important it is to have dreams. As you guide students through these topics, consider their varying world views as they share their experiences and make connections to their own lives.

The pages in this unit are reproducible. Reproduce the unit in its entirety or choose the pages that you wish to have your students do. A suggested teaching path is below.

1. **Read the Nonfiction Story (pages 12 and 13)**
   Distribute one copy of the story to each student. Have students read the text independently or read the text aloud as they follow along silently.

2. **Your Dream Job (page 14)**
   Distribute one copy of the page to each student. Guide students in completing the page independently.

3. **Let's Talk About Wes Studi (page 15)**
   Distribute one copy of the page to each student. Facilitate a whole-group discussion or divide the class into small groups.

   Prepare for discussion:
   Guide students through reading each question. Give them time to think of their answers and to write them if they want to. Then facilitate a group discussion, encouraging students to share their thoughts.

4. **Talk with Your Partner and Ideas for Your Partner (pages 16 and 17)**
   Divide students into groups of two. Distribute one copy of each page to each group. Have each group work on the activities together.

5. **Choose Your Project—Dream Big (pages 18–22)**
   Distribute one copy of the project menu to each student. Explain to students that they will each choose a project to do. After students have chosen their project, collect the project menus. Reproduce and distribute the following project pages for each student based on the student's choice:
   - Pages 19 and 20 for Dream Big—Painting
   - Pages 21 and 22 for Dream Big—Poster
   Decide whether or not students will share their finished projects with the class and instruct students accordingly.

Wes Studi's Story

Kathy Hutchins / Shutterstock.com

Wes Studi is a Cherokee American actor. He was the first Indigenous American to win an Oscar, which is an award for acting in a movie. Wes waited many years to be an actor. It was his dream to be an actor. His dream came true.

Wes was born in Nofire Hollow, Oklahoma, in 1947. His mom was a housekeeper. His dad was a ranch hand who worked with animals.

When Wes was young, he watched movies. There were few movies with Indigenous American actors. Wes wondered why those actors only played the roles of Indigenous Americans. They didn't play the roles of police officers or race car drivers. Wes had a dream to be in movies one day, but he hoped that he could play many different roles.

When Wes grew up, he became a soldier. He fought in a war. Then he worked as a horse trainer for many years.

Wes never forgot his dream of becoming a movie actor, though. He started acting in the theaters in Oklahoma. One day, he decided to move to Los Angeles to try acting in movies.

In Hollywood, Wes got some small acting jobs. Then he got lucky. He was hired to act in the movie *Dances with Wolves* in 1990. A lot of people saw the movie, and they liked it. After that, Wes got a lot more movie roles. He also started to act in TV shows.

Wes played different kinds of roles. He even played Indigenous American roles, just like the actors he used to watch as a child. He says that he likes playing Indigenous Americans because they are an important part of America's story, in the past and now.

In 2019, Wes won an Academy Award, or an Oscar. He was 71 years old when he won this award. An Indigenous American had never won an Academy Award before him.

Wes had always dreamed of becoming an actor, and he found out that dreams do come true if you never give up and you keep trying.

Name _____

Your Dream Job

Wes Studi always wanted to be an actor, but he had to do other jobs first. Still, he never gave up on his dream job of becoming an actor.

Answer the items below.

1. Draw a picture that shows what you dream of doing for a job when you grow up.

2. Wes's dream to be an actor came true. Do you think your dream can come true? Circle your answer.

yes   **maybe**   **no**

3. How would you feel if you had to do a different job until you got your dream job? Color the face that shows how you may feel.

happy   **okay**   **sad**

Name _____

Let's Talk About Wes Studi

Read the questions. Think about what you read about Wes Studi.
Think about your answers. Then you will talk with your classmates.

What do you think is important about Wes Studi?

What question would you like to ask Mr. Studi?

Do you know other people who have a dream job?
Who are they? What are their dream jobs?

Name _____

Name _____

Talk with Your Partner

Wes Studi always wanted to be an actor. After many years, his dream came true.
You don't have to wait to be a grown-up for your dreams to come true. Your
dreams can be big or small. Talk with your partner about dreams you want to
come true. Write both of your big and small dreams in the shapes.

Big and Small Things
We Dream of Coming True

Big Dream

Big Dream

Small Dream

Small Dream

Name _____

Name _____

Ideas for Your Partner

You and your partner talked about dreams that you want to come true.

Draw to show one thing your partner may try to do so his or her dream can come true. For example, Wes Studi started acting at a theater. That helped his dream come true. He became a movie actor.

This is something you might do to help your dream come true.

This is something you might do to help your dream come true.

Name _____

Choose Your Project Dream Big

Wes Studi had a dream to become a movie actor, and he did become a movie actor.

1. Think about your dream for when you grow up. Then choose a project to do.

2. Draw an **X** in the box next to the project you chose. Then give this page to your teacher.

 Paint a Picture

Paint a picture that shows what your dream job is.

 Make a Poster with Words

Make a poster that tells and shows what your dream job is.

Culturally Responsive Lessons and Activities • EMC 8262 • © Evan-Moor Corporation

Dream Big—Painting

Paint a picture. Show the job you dream of doing.

What You Need

- a sheet of light-colored construction paper
- page 20
- paints
- paintbrush
- scissors

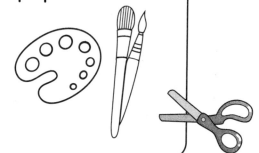

What You Do

1. You can paint your own picture, or you can use the shapes on page 20 to help you.

   First, cut out a shape. Next, put it on the construction paper. Then use your paint and paintbrush to trace around the shape. Last, take the shape off the construction paper.

2. Let your painting dry.

3. Show your painting to your friends.

Name _____

Dream Big—Poster

Make a poster with words and pictures. Show the job you dream of doing.

What You Need

- a large sheet of light-colored construction paper
- page 22
- crayons or markers
- scissors
- glue
- things to decorate a poster, such as dried pasta, beads, buttons, cotton balls, paint, glitter, pompoms, dried leaves, foil, etc.

What You Do

1. You can make your own pictures for your poster. Or you can color and cut out the pictures on page 22 and glue them onto your poster.

2. Write words to tell about your dream job.

3. Show your poster to your friends.

Name _____

Culturally Responsive Lessons and Activities • EMC 8262 • © Evan-Moor Corporation

Other People Can't Stop You

Susan Boyle's Story

This unit is about doing your best, even when other people say hurtful things or do not believe in you. Students will read about Susan Boyle, a British singer who was bullied as a child. Unfortunately, many students have experiences with bullying or may have witnessed it, so they may connect to Susan's story, or they might learn more about how to do their best even if others do not fully support them. This unit provides an opportunity for students to empathize with someone who is being bullied. As you guide students through these topics, consider their varying world views as they share their experiences and make connections to their own lives.

The pages in this unit are reproducible. Reproduce the unit in its entirety or choose the pages that you wish to have your students do. A suggested teaching path is below.

1. **Read the Nonfiction Story (pages 24 and 25)**
   Distribute one copy of the story to each student. Have students read the text independently or read the text aloud as they follow along silently.

2. **You Can Do Your Best (page 26)**
   Distribute one copy of the page to each student. Guide students in completing the page independently.

3. **Let's Talk About Susan Boyle (page 27)**
   Distribute one copy of the page to each student. Facilitate a whole-group discussion or divide the class into small groups.

   Prepare for discussion:
   Guide students through reading each question. Give them time to think of their answers and to write them if they want to. Then facilitate a group discussion, encouraging students to share their thoughts.

4. **Talk with Your Partner and Cheer Your Partner On (pages 28 and 29)**
   Divide students into groups of two. Distribute one copy of each page to each group. Have each group work on the activities together.

5. **Choose Your Project—Do Your Best (pages 30–34)**
   Distribute one copy of the project menu to each student. Explain to students that they will each choose a project to do. After students have chosen their project, collect the project menus. Reproduce and distribute the following project pages for each student based on the student's choice:
   - Pages 31 and 32 for Do Your Best—Painting
   - Pages 33 and 34 for Do Your Best—Notebook Cover
   Decide whether or not students will share their finished projects with the class and instruct students accordingly.

Name _____

Susan Boyle's Story

Music has always been an important part of Susan Boyle's life. She became one of Britain's best singers. But becoming a famous singer was not easy for Susan.

Susan was born in Scotland. She is the youngest of nine children. When she went to school, she had a hard time. She usually did not get good grades. Some of her teachers thought that she had trouble learning. Some of her classmates called her mean names.

But Susan did not let bullying stop her from singing. At age 12, Susan started singing in musicals at her school. The teachers heard how good she was. They saw her talent and love for music. They told Susan to keep singing. Her teachers believed in her.

After she left high school, Susan kept singing. She sang in church choirs. She also sang at a big festival in Scotland. Her voice kept getting better and better.

But when Susan's mom and sister got sick, Susan stopped going places to sing. She stayed home to take care of them.

In 2008, Susan decided it was time to sing again. Her mom wanted her to try out for a TV show called **Britain's Got Talent**. The winner would get to record songs with a music company, and the songs would play on the radio. Susan tried to see if **Britain's Got Talent** would let her try out. They said yes!

When Susan went onstage to sing, some people laughed when they saw her. Susan had gray hair. She was older than a lot of other people on the show. The judges thought she would be a terrible singer. They did not believe in her.

Then Susan began to sing. Her voice was strong and beautiful. Everyone stopped and listened. When she finished singing, people stood up. They all cheered loudly.

Susan didn't win "Britain's Got Talent." But she did get many singing jobs after that and became famous. She has sold millions of music albums. Now people around the world know her name.

Susan said, "If you want something bad enough, you keep going. It doesn't matter your age or anything else."

Name _____

You Can Do Your Best

Susan Boyle kept singing because she liked it, even when other people laughed at her. She didn't let other people stop her from doing her best.

Think about what you're good at. Answer the items below.

1. Draw pictures of two activities you are good at doing.

2. How do you feel when you do these activities?
Color in the shape that describes how you feel.

joyful   proud   talented

Culturally Responsive Lessons and Activities • EMC 8262 • © Evan-Moor Corporation

Name _____

Let's Talk About Susan Boyle

Read the questions. Think about what you read about Susan Boyle.
Think about your answers. Then you will talk with your classmates.

What do you think it means to "do your best"?

How do you think Susan felt when people laughed at her or treated her unkindly?

People sometimes bully others. Have you been bullied or seen others bullied? How did you feel when it happened?

Name _____

Name _____

Talk with Your Partner

Children said mean things to Susan Boyle when she was young. It's important to stand up for yourself if someone is unkind. Talk with your partner about how you can stand up for yourself using kind words. Write your reply in the speech bubble.

How Can You Stand Up for Yourself?

Someone might say...

You're not very good at this.

You can reply and say...

I believe in myself. I'm proud of my hard work.

Someone might say...

I don't want to be your friend.

You can reply and say...

Culturally Responsive Lessons and Activities • EMC 8262 • © Evan-Moor Corporation

Name _____

Name _____

Cheer Your Partner On

You and your partner talked about how to stand up for yourself. To do our best, though, it helps to have people cheering us on. For example, Susan Boyle had teachers who believed in her. They told her to keep going and keep singing.

1. Ask your partner about an activity he or she is good at.

2. Draw a picture to show one way you can cheer on your partner as your partner does his or her best at an activity.

This is one way I can cheer you on as you do your best.

This is one way I can cheer you on as you do your best.

Name _____

Choose Your Project
Do Your Best

Some people did not believe in Susan Boyle, but she always did her best.

1. Think about activities where you do your best.
Then choose a project to do.

2. Draw an **X** in the box next to the project you
chose. Then give this page to your teacher.

Paint a Picture

Paint a picture that shows
you doing your best at
an activity you love to do.

Make a Notebook Cover

Make a notebook cover with
words to cheer you on when
you want to do your best.

Do Your Best—Painting

Paint a picture of you doing your best at one of your favorite activities.

What You Need

- a large sheet of construction paper
- page 32
- paints
- paintbrush
- scissors
- glue

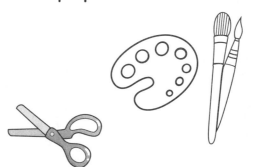

What You Do

1. You can paint your own pictures, or you can use the shapes on page 32 to help you.

   Choose a shape and cut it out. Then put it on the construction paper.

2. Use your paintbrush and paint to color the shape.

3. Glue the shape to your construction paper.

4. Paint a picture of yourself next to the shape.

5. Let your painting dry.

6. Show your painting to your friends.

Name ______________________________

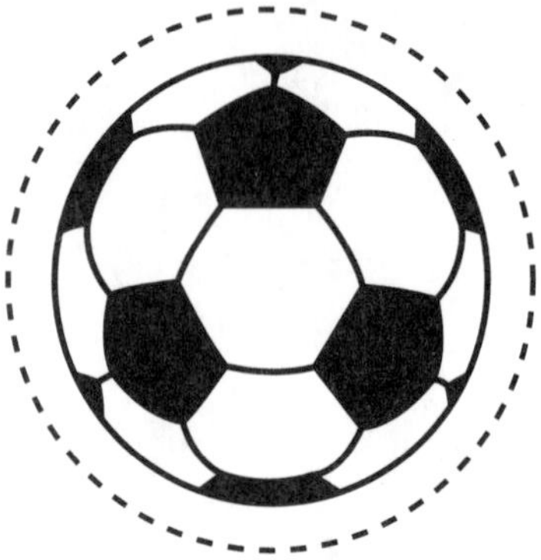

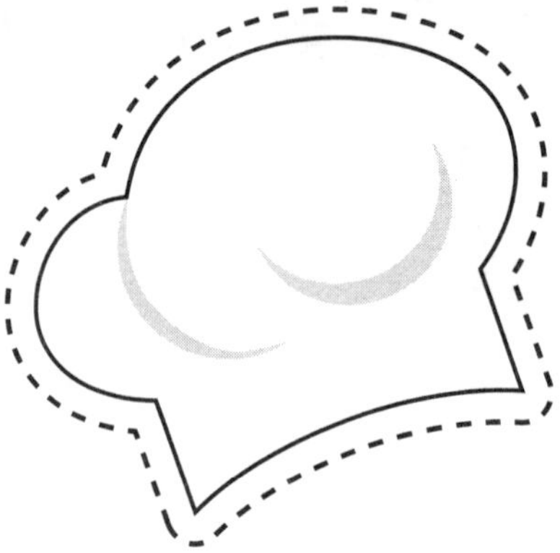

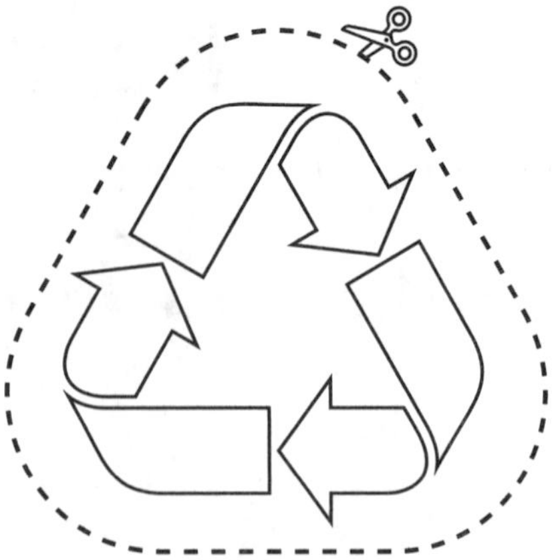

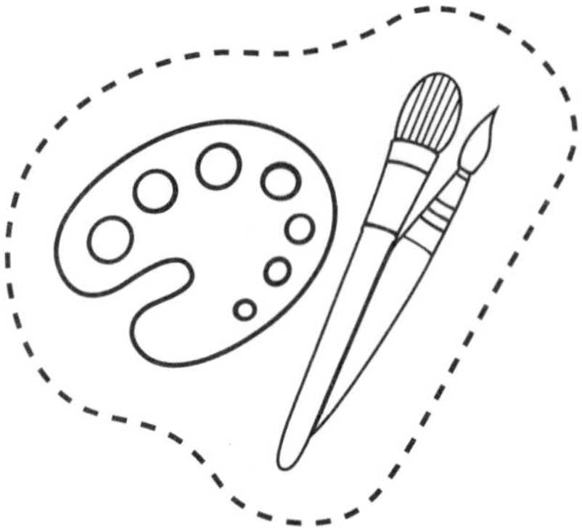

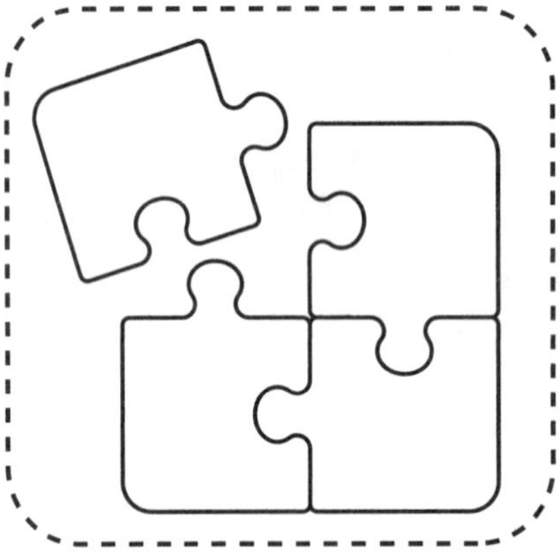

I love writing.

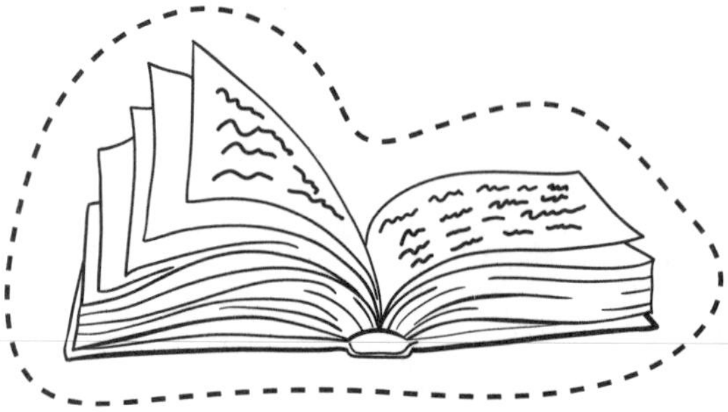

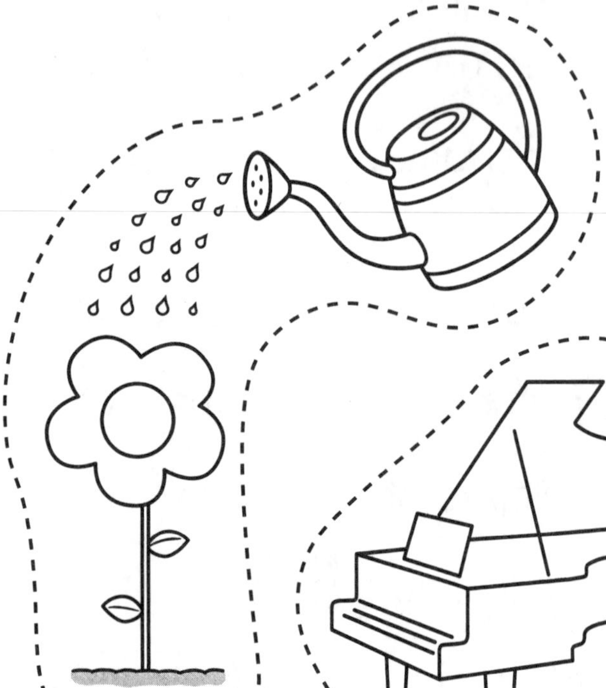

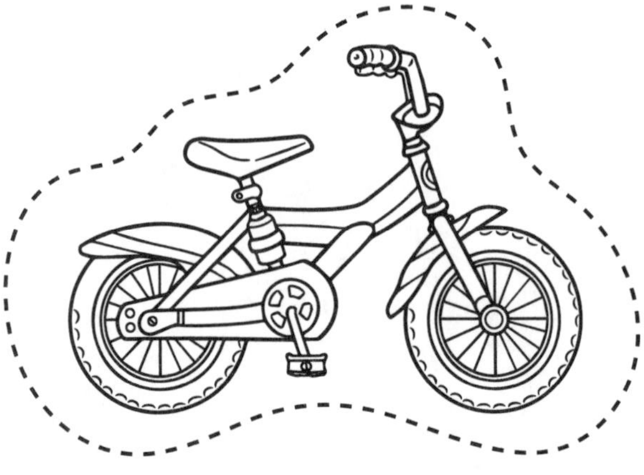

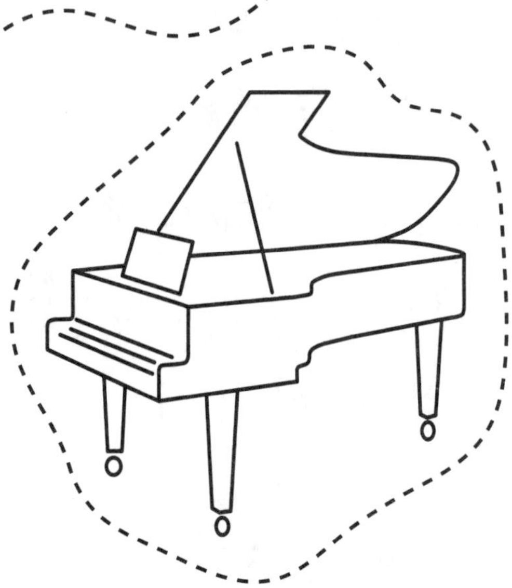

Name _____

Do Your Best—Notebook Cover

Make a notebook cover with words to remind you to do your best.

What You Need

- a sheet of construction paper
- page 34
- crayons or markers
- scissors
- glue or tape
- things to decorate the notebook cover, such as dried pasta, beads, buttons, cotton balls, paint, glitter, pompoms, dried leaves, foil, etc.

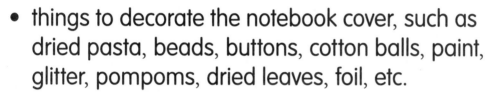

What You Do

1. Put words onto the construction paper. You can write your own words for your notebook cover. Or you can cut out and color the words on page 34 and glue them to your cover.

2. After you put words on your notebook cover, decorate it.

3. Glue or tape the construction paper onto a notebook.

4. Show your notebook cover to your friends.

I Can Do This!

NO ONE CAN STOP ME

I STAND UP FOR MYSELF

I Believe in Me

I Will Do My Best

Culturally Responsive Lessons and Activities • EMC 8262 • © Evan-Moor Corporation

Learning Helps You Do Great Things

Mikaila Ulmer's Story

This unit is about how learning can be transformative. Learning new things can open doors to amazing opportunities. Students will read about Mikaila Ulmer, a girl who overcame her fear of bees and started a business that helped them. Mikaila Ulmer's story shows how keeping an open mind through learning can sometimes help replace fear with valuable information. Learning empowers people of all ages to make choices that can help others and change the world. As you guide students through these topics, consider their varying world views as they share their experiences and make connections to their own lives.

The pages in this unit are reproducible. Reproduce the unit in its entirety or choose the pages that you wish to have your students do. A suggested teaching path is below.

1. **Read the Informational Fiction Story (pages 36 and 37)**
   Distribute one copy of the story to each student. Have students read the text independently or read the text aloud as they follow along silently.

2. **We Can All Do a Lot (page 38)**
   Distribute one copy of the page to each student. Guide students in completing the page independently.

3. **Let's Talk About Mikaila Ulmer (page 39)**
   Distribute one copy of the page to each student. Facilitate a whole-group discussion or divide the class into small groups.

   Prepare for discussion:
   Guide students through reading each question. Give them time to think of their answers and to write them if they want to. Then facilitate a group discussion, encouraging students to share their thoughts.

4. **Talk with Your Partner and Learning About Your Partner (pages 40 and 41)**
   Divide students into groups of two. Distribute one copy of each page to each group. Have each group work on the activities together.

5. **Choose Your Project—I Want to Learn (pages 42–46)**
   Distribute one copy of the project menu to each student. Explain to students that they will each choose a project to do. After students have chosen their project, collect the project menus. Reproduce and distribute the following project pages for each student based on the student's choice:
   • Pages 43 and 44 for I Want to Learn—Journal Entry
   • Pages 45 and 46 for I Want to Learn—Poster
   Decide whether or not students will share their finished projects with the class and instruct students accordingly.

Mikaila Ulmer's Story

"Mmm, this lemonade is so good!" said Esparanza. "It's my favorite."

"Well, do you know who makes this lemonade?" her mom asked. "It's a kid!"

"No way!" said Esparanza. She couldn't believe it.

Mikaila with her lemonade

Esparanza's mom looked up the lemonade online. "A girl named Mikaila started this lemonade company."

"Why is it called Me & the Bees?" asked Esparanza.

"The lemonade has honey to make it taste sweet. The bees made the honey. Mikaila's company gives money to people who help honeybees."

Esparanza made a face. "Help the bees? Why would she do that? Bees are so scary! I got stung one time, remember?"

Esparanza's mom quietly read online for a moment. Then she said, "You know what? Mikaila used to be afraid of bees, too. She got stung two times! But instead of being afraid of bees, she wanted to learn more about them."

Name _____

Mikaila helping bees

"Are honeybees in trouble?" Esparanza asked. Her mom said that honeybees are in danger. They are losing their homes. They help Earth's plants and animals. They help people, too. They move pollen and help plants grow.

"When Mikaila learned more about bees, she cared about them. She wanted to help them. She wasn't afraid of them anymore."

Esparanza and her mom read more about Mikaila. She got her lemonade recipe from her Great-Grandma Helen. And Mikaila wrote a book. She's an author! She also travels a lot. She tells people what it's like to be a kid who started a business. She won contests for kids who have business ideas because people loved her idea.

"Wait, so that means I could start a business if I have an idea?" asked Esparanza. "I could enter a kids' contest, too?"

"Of course!" said her mom. "That's how Mikaila got started!"

"That is so cool!" said Esparanza. "I have to go to my room now, Mom. I have to think of an idea for my company!" Esparanza took her bottle of lemonade and ran up to her room.

Name _____

We Can All Do a Lot

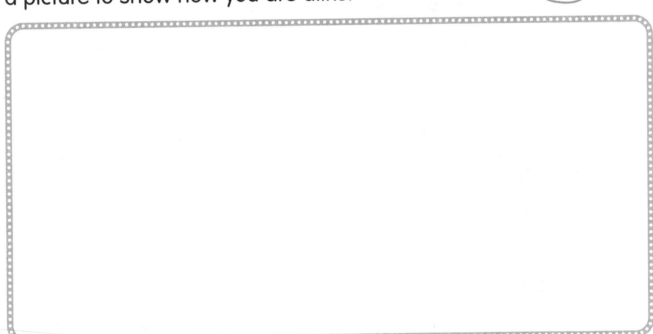

Mikaila Ulmer's story is a true story. Mikaila was afraid of bees until she learned about how they help Earth and people. What she learned helped her become a kid who started a business!

Think about the story you read. Then answer the items below.

1. How are you and Mikaila alike? Write to tell or draw a picture to show how you are alike.

2. What questions would you like to ask Mikaila? Write your questions in the speech bubbles.

Name _____

Let's Talk About Mikaila Ulmer

Read the questions. Think about what you read about Mikaila Ulmer. Think about your answers. Then you will talk with your classmates.

Mikaila's work helps bees. If you could make money to help others, who or what would you try to help? Why?

Mikaila used her Great-Grandma Helen's recipe to start her lemonade business. Is there something in your family that you would want to use to start a business?

Would you ever want to enter a contest to start a business? Why or why not?

Name _____

Name _____

Talk with Your Partner

Mikaila chose to learn about bees, and this helped her to start liking them. People like many different things. Write or draw to tell one thing you and your partner each like that is different from one another. Then write or draw to tell one thing you both like. When you're finished, talk about more things you both like!

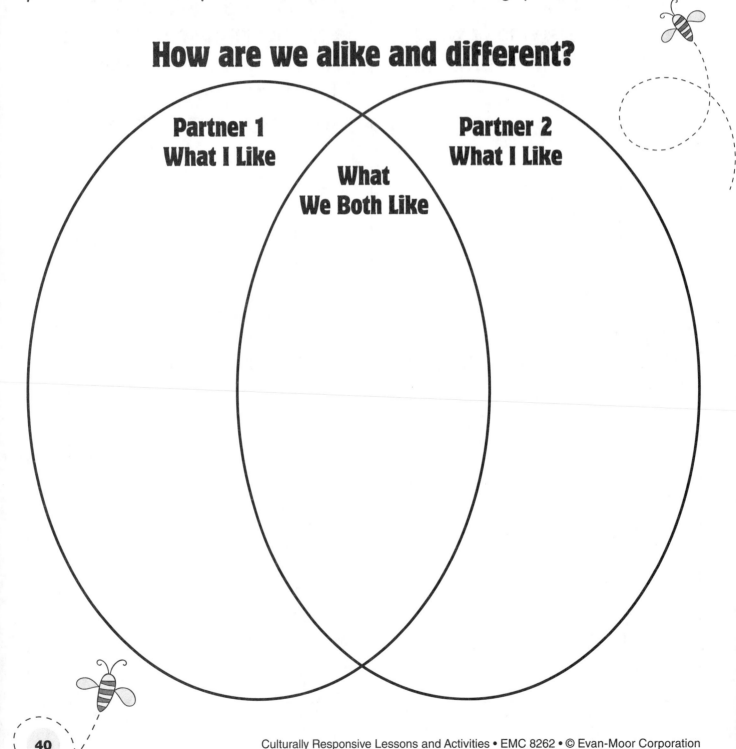

How are we alike and different?

Partner 1
What I Like

What
We Both Like

Partner 2
What I Like

Name _____

Name _____

Learning About Your Partner

You and your partner talked about things you both like.

1. Cut out the cards below. Each partner gets a card that says **Draw** and a card that says **Write** .

2. Draw a picture to show one new thing you learned about your partner.

3. On the other card, write one question you have for your partner.

4. Give the cards to your partner.

Draw This is something I learned about you today.

Draw This is something I learned about you today.

Write This is a question I have for you:

_____

_____

_____

Write This is a question I have for you:

_____

_____

_____

Choose Your Project
I Want to Learn

After Mikaila Ulmer got stung by bees, she could have chosen to dislike bees for the rest of her life. But she chose to learn more about them. This helped her do work to help the bees.

1. Think about what you want to learn more about. Then choose a project to do.

2. Draw an **X** in the box next to the project you chose. Then give this page to your teacher.

☐ **Write a Journal Entry**

Write a journal entry about something you want to learn more about.

☐ **Make a Poster**

Make a poster that tells why you want to learn more about something.

I WANT TO LEARN ABOUT

I Want to Learn—Journal Entry

Write a journal entry about what you want to learn more about.

What You Need

- a sheet of lined paper
- a sheet of white paper
- a pencil
- markers or crayons
- scissors
- glue or tape
- a paperclip or stapler
- page 44

What You Do

1. On the lined paper, write to tell something you want to learn more about. Write to tell why you want to learn about it. What will you do after you learn more? Will you try to help Earth and other people, like Mikaila Ulmer?

2. On the white paper, draw to show what you want to learn about. You might choose to cut out and paste pictures from page 44 in your drawing.

3. Use the paperclip or stapler to attach the journal pages together.

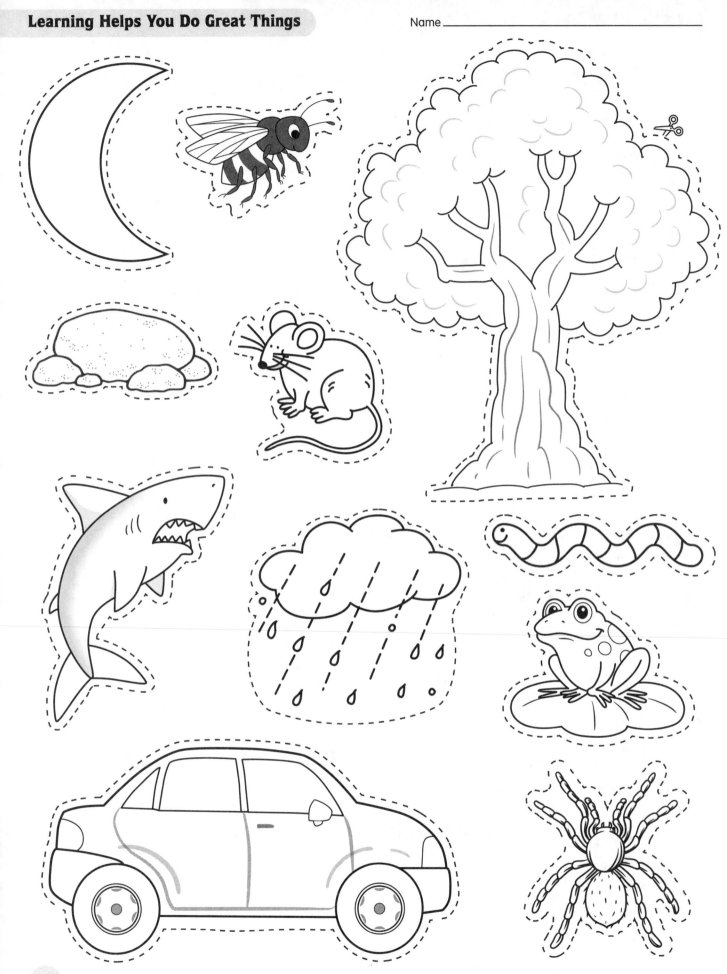

Name _____

I Want to Learn—Poster

Make a poster with words and pictures to tell what you want to learn more about.

What You Need

- a large sheet of light-colored construction paper
- page 46
- crayons or markers
- scissors
- glue
- things to decorate a poster, such as dried pasta, beads, buttons, cotton balls, paint, glitter, pompoms, dried leaves, foil, etc.

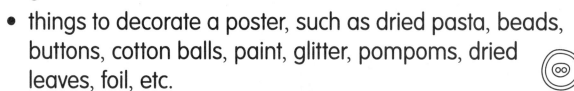

What You Do

1. Draw and write on the construction paper. Tell what you want to learn more about and why. Do you want to help Earth and other people like Mikaila Ulmer?

You can make your own words or sentences for your poster. Or you can cut out and color the sentences on page 46. You can glue them to your poster.

2. Decorate your poster.

Name _____

I want to help!

LEARNING IS FUN!

Facts can help me do better!

The more I know, the more I can do!

Learning helps me to help others!

Culturally Responsive Lessons and Activities • EMC 8262 • © Evan-Moor Corporation

You Are Never Too Young to Help

Sidney Keys III's Story

This unit is about how you are never too young to help and make a difference in your community. It is also about making the change that you want to see in the world. Sidney Keys III was a 10-year-old boy with a stutter who loved reading, and he realized that black culture and African American literature were underrepresented in his book choices. He wanted to connect with other boys in the black community, and in doing so, he became the founder and CEO of Books N Bros and a young leader. This unit is about recognizing that you can make a difference and give back to your community at any age. As you guide students through these topics, consider their varying world views as they share their experiences and make connections to their own lives.

The pages in this unit are reproducible. Reproduce the unit in its entirety or choose the pages that you wish to have your students do. A suggested teaching path is below.

1. **Read the Nonfiction Story (pages 48 and 49)**
   Distribute one copy of the story to each student. Have students read the text independently or read the text aloud as they follow along silently.

2. **How I Help (page 50)**
   Distribute one copy of the page to each student. Guide students in completing the page independently.

3. **Let's Talk About Sidney Keys III (page 51)**
   Distribute one copy of the page to each student. Facilitate a whole-group discussion or divide the class into small groups.

   Prepare for discussion:
   Guide students through reading each question. Give them time to think of their answers and to write them if they want to. Then facilitate a group discussion, encouraging students to share their thoughts.

4. **Talk with Your Partner and How We Can Help Partner Activity (pages 52 and 53)**
   Divide students into groups of two. Distribute one copy of each page to each group. Have each group work on the activities together.

5. **Choose Your Project—You Can Help (pages 54–58)**
   Distribute one copy of the project menu to each student. Explain to students that they will each choose a project to do. After students have chosen their project, collect the project menus. Reproduce and distribute the following project pages for each student based on the student's choice:
   - Pages 55 and 56 for You Can Help—Dance
   - Pages 57 and 58 for You Can Help—Flier

   Decide whether or not students will share their finished projects with the class and instruct students accordingly.

Sidney Keys III's Story

When Sidney Keys III was only 10 years old, he started a club. It was a book club called Books N Bros. Sidney started the club because he wanted to talk about books he loves with other boys from the African American community. The club was online, so the kids in the club lived in many different places. Sidney and the other kids met by

A boy doing a video chat

doing video chats. At first the club had only 7 members, but that changed quickly! Soon there were 30 kids in the club. And then there were hundreds of kids!

Sidney says that he used to speak with a stutter in elementary school. Sometimes he wanted to forget about his stutter, so he would read books. He loved books. He wanted to talk to other kids who loved books. He also wanted to help other African American kids to read more.

Sidney said that sometimes it was hard to find books about black culture. He couldn't find books about kids who were like him. He couldn't find pictures of kids who looked like him in books. This was another reason why he started Books N Bros. He wanted to talk to other kids about the books they loved reading.

Sidney had no idea that starting a book club would lead to becoming a business owner, but it did! Books N Bros is a company, and Sidney is the boss. His mom helped him start the company. Books N Bros makes money, but they do not keep all of it. They give some of the money they make to the community. Sidney wants to help as many kids as he can. He wants other kids to read more and start companies, too.

Sidney used to worry about talking in front of people because of his stutter. But he cared so much about Books N Bros and wanted to tell people about it. So he got used to talking in front of thousands of people! Sidney has been on many TV shows to talk about Books N Bros. And Marvel made a comic book about Sidney! Sidney said, "I always wanted to read books that had characters that looked like me, but I never thought that I'd see a comic book with me in it."

Sidney is writing his own book, so he is an author, too. Sidney wants kids in the black community and all kids to know that they can start a business and be leaders. He is a kid making a big difference!

Sidney Keys III

Name _____

How I Help

Sidney Keys III was 10 years old when he started to help people in his community. Even though he was a kid, he found out that he could do a lot to help other people.

Write or draw to tell 4 ways you help others.

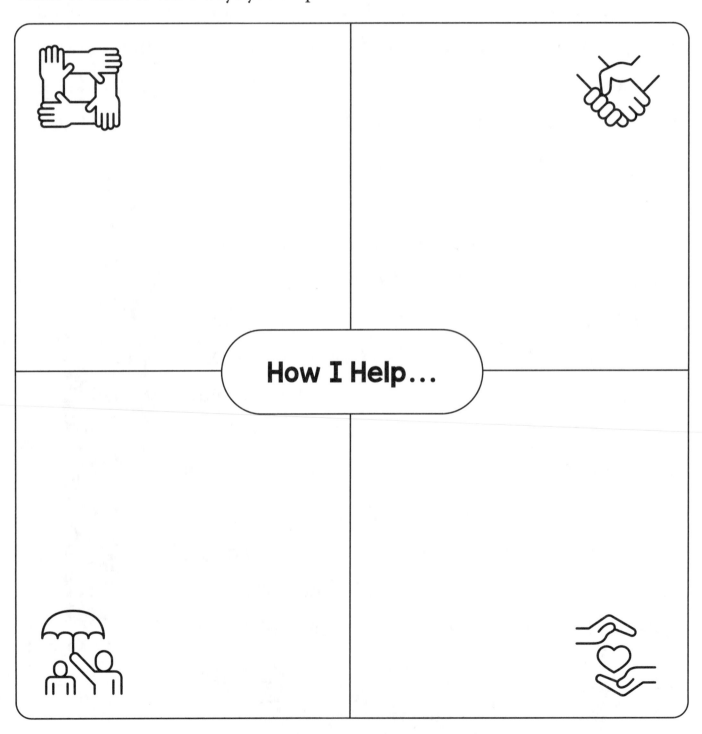

How I Help...

Name _____

Let's Talk About Sidney Keys III

Read the questions. Think about what you read about Sidney Keys III. Think about your answers. Then you will talk with your classmates.

How are you and Sidney alike?

Do you think Sidney would be a good friend? Why or why not?

Do you know anyone who is young and helps other people? Tell how they help. Or tell ways that you wish you could help other people.

Name _____

Name _____

Talk with Your Partner

Sidney Keys III wanted to help people in his community talk to each other about books. He wanted to help other kids to read more. Like Sidney, you don't have to be a grown-up to help out. Talk with your partner about problems in your community.

Are there people who do not have enough food to eat? 	Are there animals who need a home? **Animal Shelter**	Is there a lot of trash in parks or other places? 

Draw and write about two more problems.

Name _____

Name _____

How We Can Help Partner Activity

You and your partner talked about problems in your community. Draw to show one way you and your partner can help. For example, Sidney Keys III started a club to bring kids together. This is how he helped others.

 I have an idea!
This is one way we can help.

 I have an idea!
This is one way we can help.

Name _____

Choose Your Project You Can Help

Sidney Keys III was a kid, and he was able to help other people. He wanted to help people read more and talk about the books they love.

1. Think about how you can help other people. Then choose a project to do.

2. Draw an **X** in the box next to the project you chose. Then give this page to your teacher.

☐ **Perform a Dance**

Create and perform a dance that you could do to raise money for a good cause.

☐ **Make a Flier**

Make a flier that tells and shows one way you can help others.

Help Others!

Name _____

You Can Help—Dance

Create and perform a dance for a good cause.

What You Need

- page 56
- a pencil
- space to move
- a device to play music
- a device to record a video

What You Do

1. On page 56, draw or make notes to plan your dance moves. Think about dance moves you can do. You may try to watch videos of people dancing to get some ideas.

2. Choose music to dance to.

3. Find a space with plenty of room for you to move around safely.

4. If you want, have someone record you dancing.

5. Perform your dance. If you recorded it, watch the video. Then show the video to your friends.

Name _____

The song I will dance to is _____.

You Can Help—Flier

Make a flier with words and pictures to tell one way you can help others.

What You Need

- a large sheet of construction paper
- page 58
- crayons or markers
- glue
- scissors
- a pencil
- things to decorate a flier, such as dried pasta, beads, buttons, cotton balls, paint, glitter, pompoms, dried leaves, foil, etc.

What You Do

1. You can draw your own pictures for your flier. Or you can cut out and color the pictures on page 58 and glue them to your flier.

2. Cut out and color your favorite pictures.

3. Write your own words to tell how you help others.

4. Add decorations to your flier.

5. Show your flier to your friends.

Name _____

Dear Ms. Inoye,

We are having a food drive at my school. Do you have any cans or dried goods you would be willing to donate? It is for a good cause, and I would really appreciate it. Thank you!

Your neighbor,
Jessica

What You Say Matters

Keenan and Scotty

This unit is about being mindful and how what you say matters, especially within friendships. Students will read a realistic fiction story about Keenan and Scotty, two best friends who sometimes say unkind things to each other. Some students might have experienced their own friendship challenges and communication issues, so they may connect to the story, or they might learn more about how much words matter. As you guide students through these topics, consider their varying world views as they share their experiences and make connections to their own lives.

The pages in this unit are reproducible. Reproduce the unit in its entirety or choose the pages that you wish to have your students do. A suggested teaching path is below.

1. **Read the Realistic Fiction Story (pages 60 and 61)**
   Distribute one copy of the story to each student. Have students read the text independently or read the text aloud as they follow along silently.

2. **Words Matter (page 62)**
   Distribute one copy of the page to each student. Guide students in completing the page independently.

3. **Let's Talk About the Story (page 63)**
   Distribute one copy of the page to each student. Facilitate a whole-group discussion or divide the class into small groups.

   Prepare for discussion:
   Guide students through reading each question. Give them time to think of their answers and to write them if they want to. Then facilitate a group discussion, encouraging students to share their thoughts.

4. **Talk with Your Partner and Kind Cards Partner Activity (pages 64 and 65)**
   Divide students into groups of two. Distribute one copy of page 64 to each student. Distribute one copy of page 65 to each group. Then have each group work on the activities together.

5. **Choose Your Project—Kind Words (pages 66–70)**
   Distribute one copy of the project menu to each student. Explain to students that they will each choose a project to do. After students have chosen their project, collect the project menus. Reproduce and distribute the following project pages for each student based on the student's choice:
   - Pages 67 and 68 for Kind Words—Comic Book
   - Pages 69 and 70 for Kind Words—Card
   Decide whether or not students will share their finished projects with the class and instruct students accordingly.

Name _____

Keenan and Scotty

Keenan and Scotty are best friends. They are both in second grade. They do things together. And they like a lot of the same things. They both eat apples at lunch. They like to watch scary movies. And they love to play sports.

Keenan loves basketball. He's the best player in his class. He moves quickly. He makes almost every shot. Scotty loves tennis. He practices all the time. But he is not as good at playing basketball. He never makes a basket.

They are playing basketball in P.E. today. "Scotty, you're not playing very well," Keenan says, laughing. Scotty pretends to laugh, too. But inside, he feels sad. He doesn't like it when people laugh at him.

Their P.E. teacher is Mr. Gomez. Mr. Gomez claps his hands. "It's time to pick partners," he says. Everyone starts to pair up. Keenan and another student pair up.

Scotty looks around for a partner. But there's no one left. Mr. Gomez sees that Scotty is alone. He says, "One group can have three people. Who wants to play with Scotty?"

Scotty looks at Keenan. But Keenan shakes his head. "You have to practice more to play with me," he says. His voice is loud. Other kids hear, and they laugh. Mr. Gomez tells Scotty to go with another group. Scotty feels hurt. He thought Keenan was his best friend.

The next day, Keenan and Scotty get on the same school bus. Every day they sit beside each other. But today is different. Scotty does not sit with Keenan.

Keenan frowns. "Scotty, come over here!" he yells. But Scotty doesn't look at him. Keenan wonders why. Later, Keenan runs over to Scotty. "Why didn't you sit with me?" he asks.

"You didn't want to play with me yesterday," Scotty says. "I thought we were friends."

"We are!" says Keenan.

Scotty shakes his head. "I don't think friends say mean things to each other. You hurt my feelings yesterday."

"I was joking around," says Keenan. "Words can't hurt."

"My mom taught me that what I say matters," Scotty replies. "And what you said did hurt my feelings."

Name _____

Words Matter

Keenan thinks words cannot hurt people. But Scotty thinks what you say matters. Answer the items below.

1. How did Scotty feel when Keenan told him they could not play together? Color the two faces that show how he felt.

happy   sad   hurt   cared for

2. How would you feel if your friend said you could not play with him or her? Write or draw to show how you would feel.

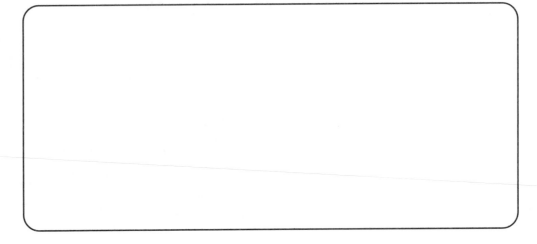

3. Why would Keenan treat his friend the way he did?
Write one reason.

_____

_____

Name _____

Let's Talk About the Story

Read the questions. Think about what you read about Keenan and Scotty. Think about your answers. Then you will talk with your classmates.

How are Scotty and Keenan alike? How are they different?

Why do you think Scotty became so upset with Keenan?

Do you think what you say matters? Or do you think that words can't really hurt anyone? Tell why.

Name _____

Talk with Your Partner

Keenan's words hurt Scotty's feelings. Talk with your partner about how you feel when you hear certain words. In the circles, write or draw how you feel.

When someone says…
"You can't play with me."

→ I feel…

When someone says…
"You're bad at this sport."

→ I feel…

When someone says…
"Let's play together!"

→ I feel…

When someone says…
"Wow, you're great at this!"

→ I feel…

Culturally Responsive Lessons and Activities • EMC 8262 • © Evan-Moor Corporation

Name _____

Name _____

Kind Cards Partner Activity

You and your partner talked about how words can make you feel. This activity can help you think about kind words. You can say these kind words to your partner and other people.

1. Cut out the cards below. Each partner will have two cards.

2. Finish the sentence on each card. Write kind words for your partner. You can also draw a picture!

3. After you finish, give the cards to your partner.

 I think you're great at...   I think you're great at...

 Thank you for...   Thank you for...

Name _____

Choose Your Project
Kind Words

Keenan and Scotty learned that what you say matters. Saying kind words is important.

1. Think about how you can speak kind words to others. Then choose a project to do.

2. Draw an **X** in the box next to the project you chose. Then give this page to your teacher.

Make a Comic Book
Make a comic book about friendship.

Make a Card
Make a card about friendship to give to someone.

Kind Words—Comic Book

Draw pictures and write words to make a comic book about friendship.

What You Need

- a sheet of construction paper
- page 68
- 3 sheets of white paper
- markers or crayons
- a pencil
- a stapler
- scissors
- glue or tape

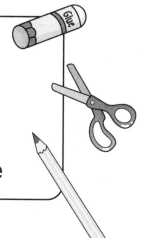

What You Do

1. Fold the construction paper in half so it opens like a book.

2. Fold the white sheets of paper in half the same way you folded the construction paper. Then put the white papers inside the construction paper. The construction paper is like a book cover, and the white sheets of paper are like the pages in the book. Staple the pages together on the left side so the pages open like a book.

3. Draw pictures of you and your friend doing things together on the white pages.

4. Write words that you and your friend say to each other on the speech bubbles on page 68. Then cut out the speech bubbles. Glue or tape them to the pictures you drew to show what you and your friend say to each other.

5. Draw a picture to decorate the comic book cover.

Name _____

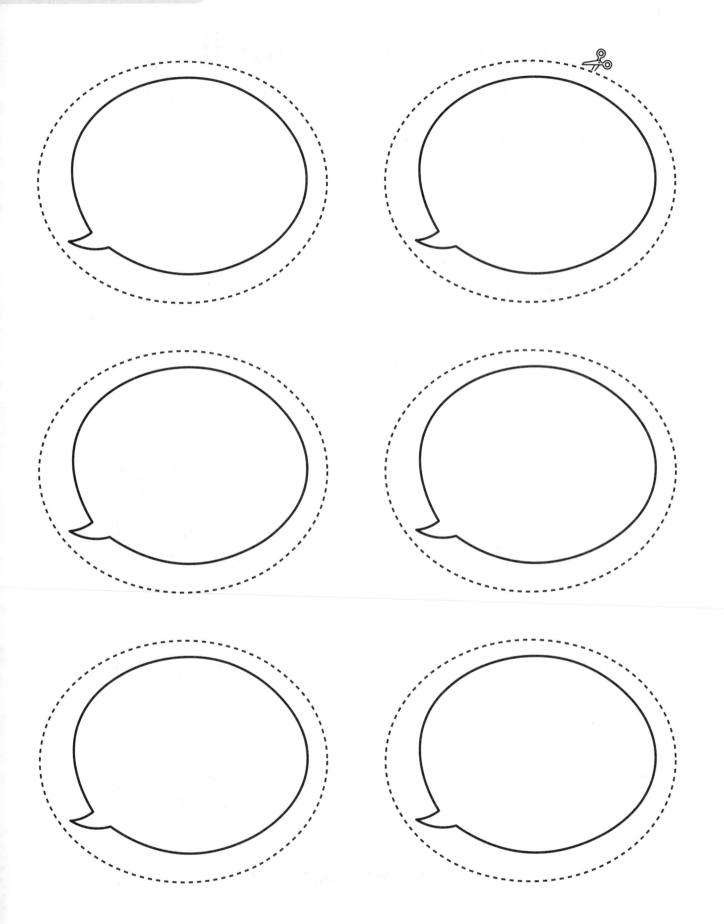

Kind Words—Card

Make a card for your friend.

What You Need

- a sheet of construction paper
- page 70
- crayons or markers
- glue or tape
- scissors
- a pencil
- materials to decorate the card, such as dried pasta, beads, buttons, cotton balls, paint, glitter, pompoms, dried leaves, foil, etc.

What You Do

1. Fold the sheet of construction paper so it opens like a birthday card.

2. You can write your own words for the card. Or you can cut out and color the words on page 70 and glue them to your card.

3. Draw pictures on the outside and inside of the card. Make sure that the words you write are kind! Write your friend's name.

4. Decorate your card.

5. Give the card to your friend.

Name _____

You Work So Hard

Thank You For Being There For Me

You Are A Great Friend

Good Job!

Let's Work Together!

You Made My Day

You Listen So Well

You Make Me Smile

Being Yourself Is Cool

Ha-Joon Can Choose for Herself

This unit is about being yourself and accepting people's differences. Students will read a realistic fiction story about Ha-Joon, a girl who stays true to herself, even when it is hard to do. Students may have struggled to feel comfortable being themselves, so they may connect to Ha-Joon's story, or they may learn anew the importance of accepting differences in themselves and others. As you guide students through these topics, consider their varying world views as they share their experiences and make connections to their own lives.

The pages in this unit are reproducible. Reproduce the unit in its entirety or choose the pages that you wish to have your students do. A suggested teaching path is below.

1. **Read the Realistic Fiction Story (pages 72 and 73)**

   Distribute one copy of the story to each student. Have students read the text independently or read the text aloud as they follow along silently.

2. **Your Favorite Foods (page 74)**

   Distribute one copy of the page to each student. Guide students in completing the page independently.

3. **Let's Talk About the Story (page 75)**

   Distribute one copy of the page to each student. Facilitate a whole-group discussion or divide the class into small groups.

   Prepare for discussion:

   Guide students through reading each question. Give them time to think of their answers and to write them if they want to. Then facilitate a group discussion, encouraging students to share their thoughts.

4. **Talk with Your Partner and What We Like Partner Activity (pages 76 and 77)**

   Divide students into groups of two. Distribute one copy of each page to each group. Have each group work on the activities together.

5. **Choose Your Project—Be Yourself (pages 78–82)**

   Distribute one copy of the project menu to each student. Explain to students that they will each choose a project to do. After students have chosen their project, collect the project menus. Reproduce and distribute the following project pages for each student based on the student's choice:
   - Pages 79 and 80 for Be Yourself—Painting
   - Pages 81 and 82 for Be Yourself—Poster

   Decide whether or not students will share their finished projects with the class and instruct students accordingly.

Name _____

Ha-Joon Can Choose for Herself

It was the first day of second grade. All the students wore nametags. Ha-Joon was sitting next to a girl named Zoe. They smiled at each other.

"Today you will make posters," said the teacher. "On your poster, tell about yourself. Draw pictures of things you like."

Ha-Joon thought for a minute. She decided to draw pictures of her favorite foods. She picked up a crayon.

Zoe frowned. "Those crayons aren't cool," said Zoe. "The markers are way better."

Ha-Joon wanted to use crayons. But she wanted Zoe to like her. So she put the crayon down. She chose a marker instead. She drew a bowl of rice. She drew a fried egg on it. Then she picked up a green marker. She drew seaweed.

"Ewww," said Zoe. "Is that seaweed? Isn't that gross? You should draw a pizza or a hamburger or something good to eat like that."

Ha-Joon felt her face get hot. She looked at her drawing.

Name _____

The food didn't look gross to her. It looked good. It made her think of her family. Eating dinner with them was her favorite part of the day. They loved to eat rice, eggs, and seaweed.

Seaweed

fried rice

Ha-Joon took a deep breath. She turned to Zoe. "I don't want to draw pizza or hamburgers," said Ha-Joon. "I want to make a poster that tells about me."

Zoe looked surprised.

"I'm Korean," said Ha-Joon. "These foods are special to me. I love to help my mom make Korean food, and I love to eat it."

"I'm sorry," said Zoe. "I didn't mean to hurt your feelings. I shouldn't have told you what to do. I really don't know what seaweed tastes like. I've never tried it."

"You should try it!" said Ha-Joon.

"Now I want to!" said Zoe. "Your picture is making me hungry!"

The girls laughed. Ha-Joon started to draw her family.

"I really like your poster," said Zoe. "I think I'll draw my family, too."

"That's a great idea!" said Ha-Joon.

Name _____

Your Favorite Foods

Ha-Joon's favorite foods are different from Zoe's. But Ha-Joon doesn't change her drawing. She is proud of her family, her culture, and her favorite foods.

Answer the items below.

1. Imagine that someone said your favorite food was gross. How would you feel? Color the face that shows your feelings.

happy   ok   sad

2. Draw a picture of your family eating dinner together. Show some of your favorite foods.

Culturally Responsive Lessons and Activities • EMC 8262 • © Evan-Moor Corporation

Name _____

Let's Talk About the Story

Read the questions. Think about what you read about Ha-Joon.
Think about your answers. Then you will talk with your classmates.

Do you think Ha-Joon
was brave in this story?
Why or why not?

Do you and your friends
like different foods from each
other? Tell an example.

What foods make you think of your family?

Name _____

Name _____

Talk with Your Partner

Ha-Joon likes seaweed. Zoe tells her to draw different foods, but Ha-Joon does not. People can like different things and still be friends. Look at the list below. Circle 3 things that you like in **RED**. Then ask your partner to circle 3 things that he or she likes in **BLUE**.

ice cream	soup	watching movies	soccer
cooking	running	singing	dancing
spiders	math	hot weather	cold weather
drawing	dogs	reading	playing with friends
science	nature	listening to music	cats
chocolate	vegetables	basketball	holidays

Culturally Responsive Lessons and Activities • EMC 8262 • © Evan-Moor Corporation

Name _____

Name _____

What We Like Partner Activity

1. Talk with your partner about the things you both like. What was the same? What was different?

2. Look at the Venn diagram. Under "Things We Both Like," write or draw things that you and your partner both like.

3. Under each part that says "Things I Like," you and your partner can write things only one of you likes.

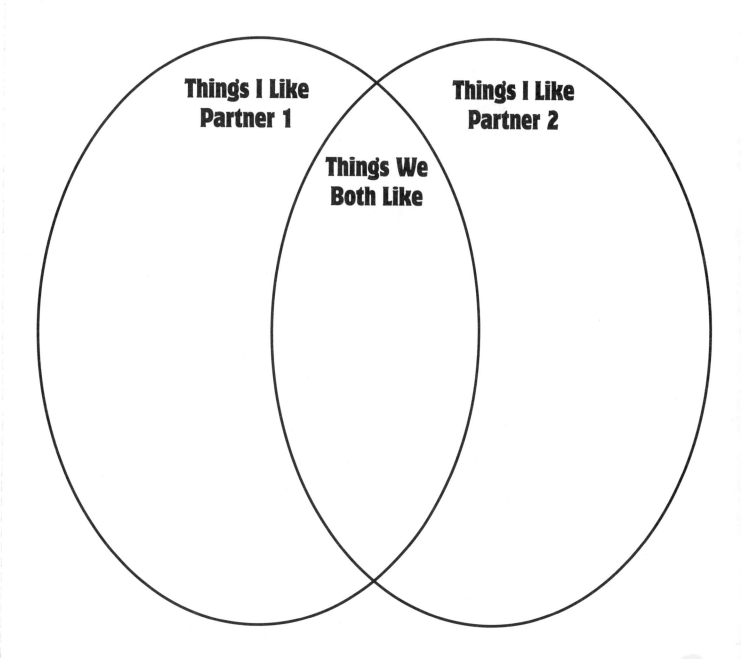

Things I Like Partner 1

Things I Like Partner 2

Things We Both Like

Name _____

Choose Your Project
Be Yourself

Ha-Joon chose to be herself and not do what other people told her to do.

1. Think about the things you like and what makes you who you are. Then choose a project to do.

2. Draw an **X** in the box next to the project you chose. Then give this page to your teacher.

☐ **Paint a Picture**

Paint a picture that shows you doing something you like.

☐ **Make a Poster with Words**

Make a poster that shows you and your family doing things you like to do together.

Name _____

Be Yourself—Painting

Paint a picture of you doing your best at one of your favorite activities.

What You Need

- a pencil
- page 80
- sheet of light-colored paper
- paint
- paintbrush

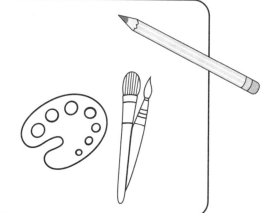

What You Do

1. On page 80, write a list of some things you like doing. Circle the one you want to paint.

2. Now paint yourself doing the activity.

3. Let your painting dry.

4. Show your painting to your friends.

Name _____

Things I Like Doing

Culturally Responsive Lessons and Activities • EMC 8262 • © Evan-Moor Corporation

Name _____

Be Yourself—Poster

Make a poster with words and pictures. Show some activities you enjoy doing with your family.

What You Need

- a pencil
- page 82
- a large sheet of light-colored construction paper
- crayons or markers
- glue
- things to decorate a poster, such as scissors, dried pasta, beads, buttons, cotton balls, paint, glitter, pompoms, magazine cut-outs, etc.

What You Do

1. On page 82, write some activities you like to do with your family. You can use one or all of these ideas in your poster.

2. Start your poster. Draw pictures that show your family doing fun activities together.

3. Write words to tell about your family's favorite activities.

4. Add decorations.

5. Show your poster to your friends.

Name _____

Things My Family Does Together

All Families Are Different

Our Families Are Different

This unit is about how all families can look different and do things differently. People can learn from seeing different kinds of families. Recognizing that there isn't one way, or a right way, to be a family is an important part of developing tolerance and fostering a feeling of respect for all people. As you guide students through these topics, keep in mind that this may be a sensitive topic for some students. Consider students' varying world views as they share their experiences and make connections to their own lives.

The pages in this unit are reproducible. Reproduce the unit in its entirety or choose the pages that you wish to have your students do. A suggested teaching path is below.

1. **Read the Realistic Fiction Story (pages 84 and 85)**
   Distribute one copy of the story to each student. Then have students read the text independently or read the text aloud as they follow along.

2. **My Family and Other Families (page 86)**
   Distribute one copy of the page to each student. Guide students in completing the page independently.

3. **Let's Talk About the Story (page 87)**
   Distribute one copy of the page to each student. Facilitate a whole-group discussion or divide the class into small groups.

   Prepare for discussion:
   Guide students through reading each question. Give them time to think of their answers and to write them if they want to. Then facilitate a group discussion, encouraging students to share their thoughts.

4. **Talk with Your Partner and Family Question Game (pages 88 and 89)**
   Divide students into groups of two. Distribute one copy of page 88 to each student. Distribute one copy of page 89 to each group. Have each group work on the activities together.

5. **Choose Your Project—Different Families (pages 90–94)**
   Distribute one copy of the project menu to each student. Explain to students that they will each choose a project to do. After students have chosen their project, collect the project menus. Reproduce and distribute the following project pages for each student based on the student's choice:
   - Pages 91 and 92 for Different Families—Book Cover
   - Pages 93 and 94 for Different Families—Paper Chain Family
   For the Paper Chain Family: Note how many people each student wrote are in his or her family. Provide the needed amount of copies of page 94 for each student. After students complete their paper chain families, collect them and tape them together to make one big paper chain family to hang in your classroom. Then invite students to talk about how each family is different.

Name _____

Our Families Are Different

It was lunch recess. Tiana and Shaniqua were swinging. Then Shaniqua remembered something that she wanted to tell Tiana. "Hey, Tiana, I saw your mom drop you off at school yesterday. I never saw her before."

"Yeah, my dad brings me to school most days," said Tiana.

Shaniqua still wanted to tell Tiana something. So she said, "I didn't know your mom was Chinese. I thought both your parents were Black like my parents are. So, are you part Chinese?"

"She's not Chinese," Tiana said quickly. "She's from Thailand. I am half Black, half Thai."

Shaniqua felt bad. "Sorry about that."

But Tiana wasn't sad or mad at all. She was smiling. "It's okay. I'm glad you asked about my family."

Shaniqua had one more question. "So, who is that older boy from the 4th grade who I see you talking to sometimes?"

Tiana laughed. "That's my brother, DaQuan."

Shaniqua smiled. "Oh, I didn't know! I thought he was Chinese. I was just wondering how you knew him."

Later, Tiana and Shaniqua were waiting for their parents to pick them up from school. Shaniqua's mom got there first. Tiana watched Shaniqua go to her mom's car and say hi. But the woman inside did not look like Shaniqua's mom. The next day, she asked Shaniqua who the woman was.

"Oh, my stepmom picked me up," said Shaniqua. "Her name is Shondra. She's really nice."

"So, do you call her Mom?" asked Tiana.

"No, I call her Shondra," said Shaniqua. "She is married to my dad. My mom lives really close to my dad and Shondra's house. So I get to see all of them a lot. I have a stepsister and a stepbrother, too. They're older."

"Your family is so different from mine!" said Tiana.

"And your family is different from mine!" said Shaniqua, smiling.

Name _____

My Family and Other Families

Shaniqua and Tiana learned that families can be different. Think about your family. Think about other families.

Answer the items below. Color the shapes or write.

1. Do you think your family is different from other families in some ways?

2. Do you ever have questions about your friends' families?

3. Write one way that your family is the same as other families.

_____

_____

_____

Name _____

Let's Talk About the Story

Read the questions. Think about the story you read about Shaniqua and Tiana. Think about your own family. Think about your answers to the questions. Then you will talk with your classmates.

What did Shaniqua and Tiana learn about families?

Do you think Tiana should have been angry when Shaniqua asked questions about her family? Why or why not?

Sometimes the people in a family do not look the same. Sometimes they do look the same.

Do you think it matters if people in a family look the same or different? Why or why not?

Name _____

Talk with Your Partner

Shaniqua and Tiana have families that look different and that do things differently. Draw a picture that shows something you and your family like to do together. Write a sentence about it. Then show the picture to your partner. Tell your partner about the picture you drew.

My family and I like to _____.

Name _____

Name _____

Family Question Game

Play a game with your partner. Read the question in each shape. Each partner should tell an answer. After both partners have answered, color the shape. Then choose another shape. The game is over when you have colored all the shapes.

Do you have a pet as part of your family? If yes, tell about it. If not, tell if you want one or not.

What is a food that your family loves to eat or make?

What are your favorite things to do with your family?

What do you do when you spend time with your cousins or friends?

Do you have sisters or brothers? If yes, tell about them. If not, do you want sisters or brothers?

What do the people in your family look like? Do they look alike or different from each other? Tell about their hair color and eye color. Tell if they have curly or straight hair. Think of other things to tell about how your family members look.

Do you have a big family?

Name _____

Choose Your Project
Different Families

Shaniqua and Tiana learned that all families can be different. They both liked their own families.

1. Think about your family and how it is different and the same as other families. Then choose a project to do.

2. Draw an **X** in the box next to the project you chose. Then give this page to your teacher.

☐ **Make a Book Cover**

Write and draw to make a cover for a book that could be about your family.

☐ **Make a Paper Chain Family**

Cut out pictures and color them to make a paper chain family that shows how your family is special!

I have _____ people in my family.

Name _____

Different Families—Book Cover

If there was a book about your family, what would it be called? What would the book be about? Write a title and draw pictures.

What You Need

- a sheet of light-colored construction paper
- page 92
- markers or crayons
- scissors
- glue or tape
- a pencil

What You Do

1. On the paper, write a title for a book about your family. You can write your own title, or you can use the **Title Idea** below to help you.

2. You can draw your own picture on the cover, or you can use the pictures on page 92 to help you.

   First, cut out a shape. Next, glue or tape it onto the paper.

3. Show your book cover to your friends.

Title Idea

The _____ _____ Family
             adjective   your family's last name

Example: The Amazing Yang Family

Name _____

Culturally Responsive Lessons and Activities • EMC 8262 • © Evan-Moor Corporation

Different Families— Paper Chain Family

Families can look different and do things differently. That is what makes a family special. Make a paper chain family that shows your special family.

What You Need

- page 94
- crayons or markers
- tape
- scissors

What You Do

1. Color and draw on the paper chain people on page 94.

   a. You can make them look like the people in your family.

   b. You can make each one a different color to show how you are all different.

   c. You can draw pictures on them. You can write words on them.

   d. You can make them look any way you want to show that your family is special.

2. After you finish coloring and decorating your paper chain family, cut them out and tape all of them together so they are holding hands.

3. Then give them to your teacher so he or she can tape them to your classmates' paper chain families and hang them up in your classroom!

Name _____

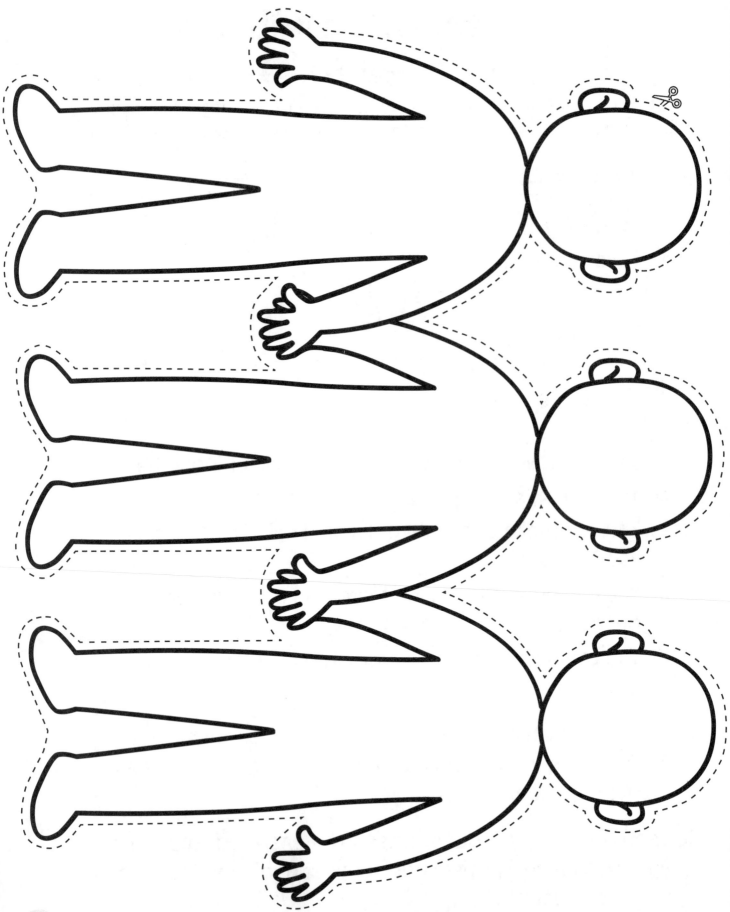

Change Can Be Hard

Two Schools Every Year

This unit is about changes that children and families go through. For some families, change can be hard because it brings difficult circumstances; for other families, change can be good and bring exciting opportunities. Students will read a realistic fiction story about Berto and Blanca, children of migrant farmworkers who move from Yuma, Arizona, to Salinas, California, in the middle of the year, causing the children to have to change schools. The students may connect to Berto and Blanca's story, or they may gain a better understanding of how hard it can be to move to a new home and a new school. As you guide students through these topics, consider their varying world views as they share their experiences and make connections to their own lives.

The pages in this unit are reproducible. Reproduce the unit in its entirety or choose the pages that you wish to have your students do. A suggested teaching path is below.

1. **Read the Realistic Fiction Story (pages 96 and 97)**

   Distribute one copy of the story to each student. Have students read the text independently or read the text aloud as they follow along.

2. **Feelings About Change (page 98)**

   Distribute one copy of the page to each student. Guide students in completing the activity independently.

3. **Let's Talk About the Story (page 99)**

   Distribute one copy of the page to each student. Facilitate a whole-group discussion or divide the class into small groups.

   Prepare for discussion:
   Guide students through reading each question. Give them time to think of their answers and to write them if they want to. Then facilitate a group discussion, encouraging students to share their thoughts.

4. **Talk with Your Partner and Which Changes Would Be Hard? (pages 100 and 101)**

   Divide students into groups of two. Distribute one copy of page 100 to each student. Distribute one copy of page 101 to each group. Have each group work on the activities together.

5. **Choose Your Project—Feelings and Changes (pages 102–106)**

   Distribute one copy of the project menu to each student. Explain to students that they will each choose a project to do. After students have chosen their project, collect the project menus. Reproduce and distribute the following project pages for each student based on the student's choice:
   - Pages 103 and 104 for Feelings and Changes—Write a Story
   - Pages 105 and 106 for Feelings and Changes—Feelings Book

   Decide whether or not students will share their finished projects with the class and instruct students accordingly.

Name _____

Two Schools Every Year

Berto ran through the fields of red strawberries. "Mamá, Mamá! I'm in the same class as Federico!" he said.

"Berto, you know you are not supposed to run onto the fields," said Mamá as she looked around her and slowly stood up. She pulled Berto to her for a hug.

"Sorry, Mamá, I just had to tell you! I'm so happy! I'll run back to the house and help Blanca make dinner. Should we make you a hot bath?" Berto knew his mamá would be sore after a long day picking strawberries. Mamá nodded and started picking strawberries again.

Berto skipped to the house with a smile on his face. He had the best first day of school ever! He finally knew someone in his class. Each year he went to two schools. His parents were migrant farm workers, so they moved from Yuma, Arizona, to Salinas, California, every year. They moved so they could be where it was picking season. Moving a lot made it hard to make friends at school.

Berto walked into their small house, which was beside the fields. It was in a row of houses that all looked the same. He saw his papá inside. "Papá, Federico from Yuma is in my class!" Berto said.

Culturally Responsive Lessons and Activities • EMC 8262 • © Evan-Moor Corporation

"Good, Mijo. I'm glad you are back with your amigo. Now go help your sister with dinner. Mamá will be home soon."

As Berto went into the small kitchen, he saw his older sister, Blanca, wiping tears from her eyes as she cut peppers. He asked what was wrong.

"It is just hard moving schools in the middle of the year," said Blanca. "I don't have anyone I know in my classes. I'll have to try and make new friends again."

Berto thought about how hard it was when he did not know anyone at his other schools. He thought about how happy he was when he saw Federico in his class today.

"I understand, Blanca," Berto said as he put his arm around his sister. "Going to two schools every year is hard. Moving from house to house is hard. Change can be hard."

Suddenly, someone was knocking at the door. Blanca opened it.

"Alma!" shouted Blanca with a smile. "I thought your family was going to Washington after you left Yuma."

"Mi padre got a job at the strawberry fields here!" said Alma.

"Well," said Berto, "change can be hard. But sometimes a change of plans can be good!"

Name _____

Feelings About Change

Berto and Blanco had many changes in their lives. They went to two schools each year. They moved to a new home two times each year. Change can be hard. Change can also bring good things, like making new friends.

Answer the items below.

1. Imagine you had to change schools two times each year. How would you feel? Color the face that shows your feelings.

happy   ok   sad

2. Have you had a new student in your class in the middle of the year? Color the shapes that tell how that student may feel.

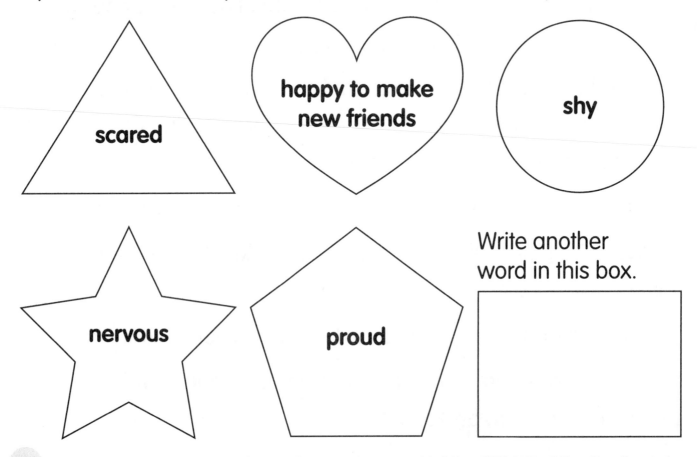

scared

happy to make new friends

shy

nervous

proud

Write another word in this box.

Culturally Responsive Lessons and Activities • EMC 8262 • © Evan-Moor Corporation

Name _____

Let's Talk About the Story

Read the questions. Think about what you read about Berto and his family and friends. Think about your answers. Then you will talk with your classmates.

Why was Berto excited that Federico was in his class?

Have you ever felt like Berto and Blanca feel about moving and going to a new school?

Berto's mamá and papá are migrant farm workers. They move to different places each year when it is time to harvest the crops.

What are some things that can be hard about this?

What are some things that can be good about this?

Name _____

Talk with Your Partner

Berto and Blanca have a lot of changes in their lives. Sometimes change can be hard. Color all of the changes you think would be hard.

Which of These Changes Would Be Hard?

you are moving to a new house	you are going to a new school	you have a new baby in your family
your school changes the lunch menu	your mom gets a new job	your best friend moves away
your dad has to work at night instead of during the day now	the library in town closes	

Culturally Responsive Lessons and Activities • EMC 8262 • © Evan-Moor Corporation

Which Changes Would Be Hard?

Write one partner's name at the top of each column. Use page 100 to compare your answers with your partner's. Then put a √ next to each of the things you colored.

Changes that would be hard	Changes that would be hard
☐ you are moving to a new house	☐ you are moving to a new house
☐ your mom gets a new job	☐ your mom gets a new job
☐ you are going to a new school	☐ you are going to a new school
☐ the library in town closes	☐ the library in town closes
☐ your best friend moves away	☐ your best friend moves away
☐ you have a new baby in your family	☐ you have a new baby in your family
☐ your dad has to work at night instead of during the day now	☐ your dad has to work at night instead of during the day now
☐ your school changes the lunch menu	☐ your school changes the lunch menu

Name _____

Choose Your Project
Feelings and Changes

Sometimes when things change, people have different feelings about those changes. Every person is different and may feel differently about changes.

1. Think about how you feel about change or how someone else may feel about change. Then choose a project to do.

2. Draw an **X** in the box next to the project you chose. Then give this page to your teacher.

☐ **Write a Story**

Write a story about a child who has a change in his or her life.

The Big Change

My friend got a new puppy. But then the...

☐ **Make a Feelings Book**

Make a book that shows how someone may feel about things that change in his or her life.

Feelings Book

Name _____

Write a Story

Write a story that has a beginning, a middle, and an end. The story will be about a child who has a change in his or her life.

What You Need

- a pencil
- page 104

What You Do

1. Plan your story in the box on this page.

2. Write your story on page 104.

3. Read your story after you are finished. Make any changes you want to.

4. Give your story to someone to read.

The main character in my story is named _____.

The change in my story is _____

_____

_____.

Name _____

A Story About Changes

Beginning

Middle

End

Name _____

Feelings Book

Make a book with words and pictures about feelings and changes.

What You Need

- a pencil
- page 106
- 3 sheets of paper
- crayons or markers

- glue
- scissors
- a stapler

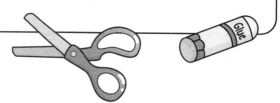

What You Do

1. Cut each sheet of paper in half. Then put the sheets of paper together and staple them on the edge. This is your book.

2. The first page is the cover. Write "Feelings Book." You can draw pictures, too. You can also write your name on it.

3. On each inside page of the book, draw or write one sentence about changes that happen to someone. For example, you can write, "This boy is going to a new school." You can cut out the feeling words and pictures on page 106 and glue them in your book, or you can draw pictures of your own.

4. These are some things you may write about:

Moving to a new house   Having a new brother or sister

Going to a new school   Losing your bike and getting a new one

Feelings Book

EXCITED

SAD

SCARED

HAPPY

SHY

MAD

We Are Together

This unit is about helping the students in your classroom understand that together, they form a community. The activities in this unit can help students think about cooperation, empathy, friendship, and diversity. As students do these activities, we hope they will think about their classmates and about other people they meet in the world. All students deserve to feel seen by their peers. Through these activities, students may reach the understanding that it can feel good to be part of a group, and a world, with diversity. The purpose of this unit is to help students understand that empathy can be a powerful tool in coming together with other people.

The pages in this unit are reproducible. Reproduce the unit in its entirety or choose the pages that you wish to have your students do.

1. **My Class Gumballs (pages 108–110)**
   You may choose to provide each student with a list of names of all students in the class. Distribute one copy of each activity page to each student. Students may need additional copies of page 109 depending on the number of students in the class. Provide students with the materials needed for this activity.

2. **How Are the Pictures Different? (page 111)**
   Distribute one copy of the page to each student.

3. **Alone or Together? (page 112)**
   Distribute one copy of the page to each student.

4. **How Do They Feel? (page 113)**
   Distribute one copy of the page to each student.

5. **Friends Letter (page 114)**
   Distribute one copy of the page to each student.

6. **Empathy Freeze Game (page 115)**
   Distribute one copy of the page to each student. Provide students with the materials needed for this activity and with space to move and dance.

7. **Working with Other People (page 116)**
   Distribute one copy of the page to each student.

8. **Balloon Time Game (page 117)**
   Distribute one copy of the page to each group of students. Provide students with the materials needed for this activity and with space to move across the room or game area.

9. **My Page in the Class Book (page 118)**
   Distribute one copy of the page to each student. Then staple all of the pages together to make a class book about every student. You may choose to create a cover page for the book.

Name _____

My Class Gumballs

It is important to know the names of all the people in your class.
Make a gumball machine that tells the names of everyone in your class.

What You Need

- pages 109 and 110
- scissors
- markers or crayons
- glue or tape
- a pencil

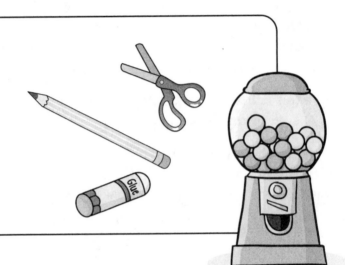

What You Do

1. Write the name of each of your classmates on the line inside each gumball circle on page 109. Make sure to write everyone's name! Then color each gumball around the person's name.

2. Cut out the gumballs. Then cut out the gumball machine on page 110.

3. Glue or tape the gumballs on the front and back of the gumball machine.

4. Show your class gumballs to your friends.

Name _____

Name _____

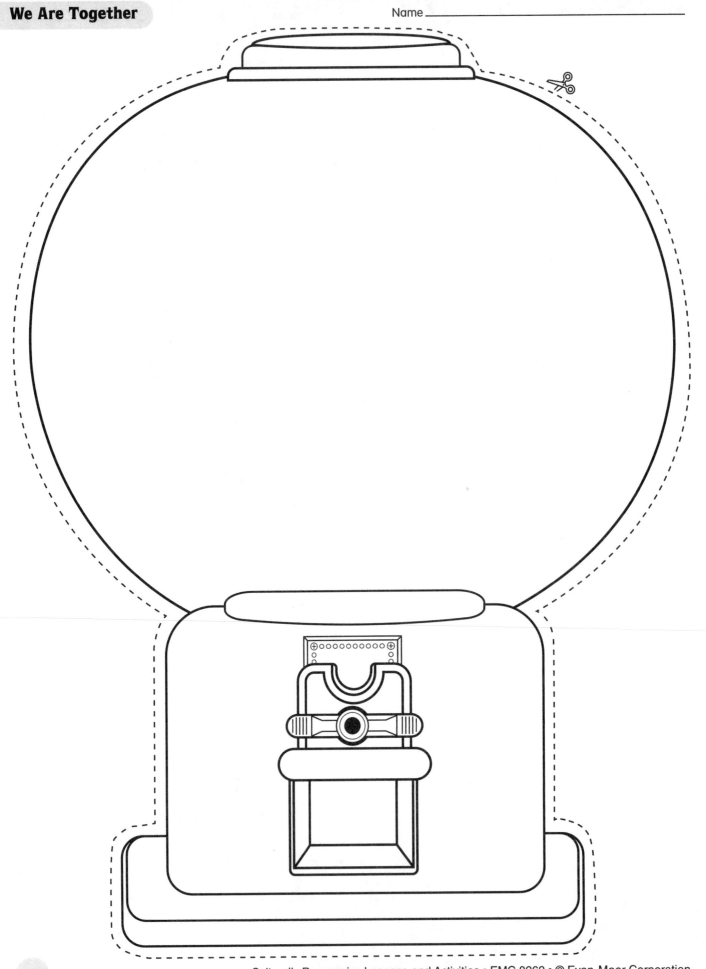

Name _____

How Are the Pictures Different?

Look at the pictures. Then write two differences between the pictures.

The pictures are different because...

_____

_____

Name _____

Alone or Together?

Sometimes people like to be alone. Sometimes they like to be with other people. Tell about how you feel.

1. I like being alone sometimes

because _____

_____

_____.

2. I like being with other people

sometimes because _____

_____.

3. It is important to be nice to other people because _____

_____.

Circle the words to finish the sentence.

4. I like it when other people

tell the truth   yell at me

play fair   push me

are nice to me   smile at me

break the rules   talk to me

Name _____

How Do They Feel?

Look at the pictures. Think about how the
kids might feel. Finish the sentences.

1. This boy's dog is lost. I would say
this to try to help him feel better:

_____

_____

_____

2. This boy's soccer team lost the game.
He didn't like losing the game. He got mad
at the other kids on his team. He said it
wasn't his fault they lost the game.

Do you think the boy is being **fair** or **unfair**?

I think the boy is being _____ because

_____

_____

_____.

Name _____

Friends Letter

Is there someone in your class whom you have not made friends with yet? All people can make new friends. Think of a person whom you would like to be friends with. Write on the lines to write a letter to that person.

_____
date

Dear _____,

     I think we could be good friends. I am a good friend because _____.

     I think one way we are different from each other is that _____

_____.

     I think one way we are the same is that

_____

_____.

     I would like to be your friend because

_____

_____.

Sincerely,

_____
your name

Culturally Responsive Lessons and Activities • EMC 8262 • © Evan-Moor Corporation

Empathy Freeze Game

Empathy means that you try to think about how someone else feels. You try to understand why they think or feel how they do.

Play a fun game and practice your empathy skills.

What You Need

- a device to play music
- at least 3 players

What You Do

1. Each player can take turns being the leader. Choose who will be the leader first.

2. The leader plays music, and the other players dance.

3. The leader chooses when to stop the music and yell **Freeze**! When the other players hear **freeze**, they must stop dancing and not move at all.

   Whoever moves after the leader yells **freeze** must sit down. Then the leader plays the music again and play continues.

4. The leader may choose to show empathy by letting 1 sitting player back in the game.

   Continue playing until only 1 player is standing.

Name

Working with Other People

Read the sentences. Then look at the pictures. Last, color the circle under the team that is working better together.

1. Both of the teams are helping to clean up garbage in the neighborhood.

Fred is mad that Quincy got the grabber tool first. Fred wanted it.

Ana told the group that she wants to help do any job.

○

○

Finish the sentence to tell why you chose this answer.

2. I chose this team because _____

_____.

Sometimes we have to work with other people to get a job done. How can you try to be helpful? Write to finish the sentence.

3. I can help my family at home by _____

_____

_____.

Culturally Responsive Lessons and Activities • EMC 8262 • © Evan-Moor Corporation

Balloon Time Game

Play a fun game with your classmates!

What You Need

- groups of 2 people
- 4 balloons for each group
- indoor space to move around
- device to keep time such as a stopwatch or smartphone
- a pencil
- a sheet of paper

What You Do

1. Choose which person in the group will play first.

2. The first player must push all balloons up into the air, then keep tapping them to keep them all in the air as long as possible. If a balloon touches the ground, it is out of the game. Time how long it takes for all balloons to touch the ground. Write the player's name and time.

3. The second player will repeat the game and see if he or she can get a longer time.

4. Both players can play at once to see if they get a longer time when they work together.

My Page in the Class Book

This page is all about ME!

My name is

_____

_____.

I like my name because

_____

_____.

This is a picture of me doing something I love to do:

I am _____ years old.

I have _____ brothers and _____ sisters.

Some of my friends are named _____,

_____, and _____.

My favorite color is _____.

My favorite food is _____.

I am a _____ friend.
write an adjective

Food and Me

This unit is about food and culture. Some people feel that they can relate to other people through food. Making food together and sharing foods can help people learn about each other. Different kinds of foods can help tell a story about who we are and what we like. Food is just one of the things that we use as a bridge to connect with other people. The activities in this unit may help support children as they think about the foods they eat and learn about the foods that their friends, families, and classmates eat. Keep in mind that food insecurity may be a very real problem for some of your students. Also, access to different kinds of foods differs for people based on geographic location and other factors. As you guide students through these topics, consider their varying world views as they share their experiences and make connections to their own lives.

The pages in this unit are reproducible. Reproduce the unit in its entirety or choose the pages that you wish to have your students do.

1. **Meals We Eat (page 120)**
   Distribute one copy of the page to each student.

2. **What's Their Favorite Food? (pages 121 and 122)**
   Distribute one copy of pages 121 and 122 to each student.

3. **Do You Want to Try a Restaurant? (page 123)**
   Distribute one copy of the page to each student. Tell students that they will need the help of an adult for this activity.

4. **Try a New Food (page 124)**
   Distribute one copy of the page to each student. Tell students that they will need the help of an adult for this activity.

5. **Me and My Food (page 125)**
   Distribute one copy of the page to each student.

6. **Circle Food Letter Game (pages 126 and 127)**
   Arrange space for students to sit in a circle. Distribute one copy of pages 126 and 127 to each student. Provide students with the materials needed for this activity.

7. **Meal Times (page 128)**
   Distribute one copy of the page to each student.

8. **Happy Popcorn Messages (pages 129 and 130)**
   Distribute one copy of pages 129 and 130 to each student. Provide students with the materials needed for this activity.

Name _____

Meals We Eat

Think about the foods that you and your family eat.

Draw or write foods you and your family eat for breakfast.

Draw or write foods you and your family eat for lunch or dinner.

Draw or write foods you and your family eat for dessert.

Name _____

What's Their Favorite Food?

Think about the foods that you eat with your family and friends. Can you guess what their favorite foods are?

1. Choose 3 people to write about. Write their names in the chart.

2. Guess what each person's favorite food is. Write your guesses in the chart.

3. Do the activity on page 122.

Names	Food Guesses

Name _____

What's Their Favorite Food? *continued*

You guessed what your family and friends' favorite foods are. Were you right?
Let's find out!

1. Ask each person you guessed about what his or her favorite
food is. Write the name of the food on the bowl.

2. Color the ☺ if you were right. Color the 💡☺ if you learned
something new.

Name _____

Do You Want to Try a Restaurant?

With a grown-up, find two restaurants that sell foods from different countries. For example, one restaurant may sell Chinese food, and another restaurant may sell French food. Write the name of each restaurant and country.

1. Do you want to try this restaurant?
Circle your answer.

yes   no

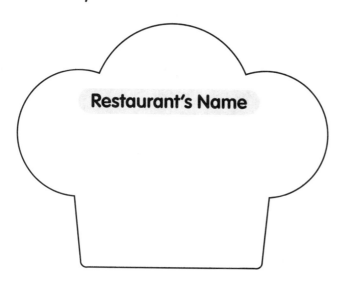

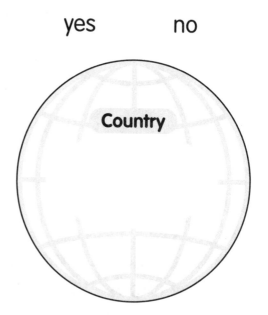

2. Do you want to try this restaurant?
Circle your answer.

yes   **no**

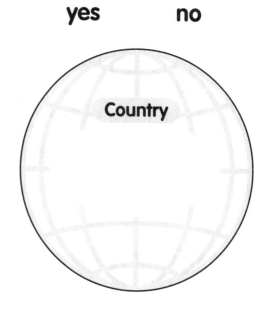

Name _____

Try a New Food

Ask a grown-up to help you try a new food that you have never eaten before. You might choose to go to a restaurant you have never been to before. You might want to help make the new food at your home. After you try the new food, tell about it.

1. Draw a picture of the new food that you tried.

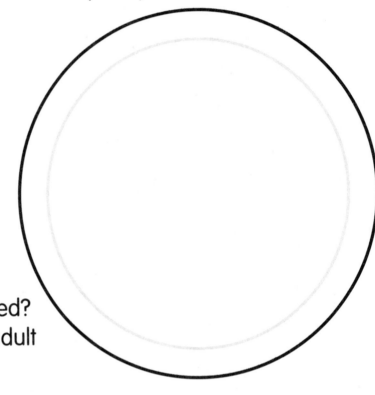

2. What was the new food called? You may choose to ask an adult to help you spell it.

_____

3. Color to answer **yes** to the questions below.
   Color to answer **no**.

Did you like this food?
_____

Would you eat this food again?
_____

Do you want your friends to try this food?

Culturally Responsive Lessons and Activities • EMC 8262 • © Evan-Moor Corporation

Name _____

Me and My Food

Different people like different kinds of food. Answer the items.

1. Write or draw a food you want to try that you have not tried yet.

2. Draw a picture of your favorite food. This food is called

_____.

3. What do you think is the worst food? Write or draw it.

Name _____

Circle Food Letter Game

This game will help you learn some of the foods that your classmates like.

What You Need

- page 127
- space for the class to sit in a circle
- a pencil

What You Do

1. Sit in a circle with all of your classmates. Use page 127 and a pencil.

2. The teacher will choose someone to go first. When it is each player's turn, the student will say a food that he or she likes that begins with the same letter of his or her name.

   For example, if your name is Lily, you might say "lemons." Or if your name is Paul, you might say "pizza."

   Write each person's name and the food he or she said on page 127.

Circle Food Letter Game, *continued*

Write each person's name and the food he or she said.

Name	Food

Name _____

Meal Times

Answer the items below.

1. Do you like to eat alone or with other people? Draw a picture to show how you like to eat.

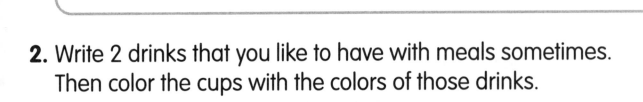

2. Write 2 drinks that you like to have with meals sometimes. Then color the cups with the colors of those drinks.

_____   _____

Name _____

Happy Popcorn Messages

Some people believe that sharing food can help people feel happy and make new friends. Some people like to eat food with friends. Write popcorn messages to someone you want to be friends with.

What You Need

- a small paper bag, about the size of a lunch bag
- page 130
- a pencil
- scissors
- materials to decorate the bag, such as glue, pompoms, beads, buttons, fabric, tape, colored tissue paper, construction paper, markers, paint, foil, sparkles, etc.

What You Do

1. Write to finish the sentences on page 130. Then cut out the rectangles.

2. Decorate the outside of the paper bag.

3. Crumple the rectangles you cut out so that they look like pieces of popcorn. Then put them inside the paper bag.

4. Give the bag to someone you would like to be friends with.

Name _____

One thing I like about you is that _____

_____

_____

_____ .

One way we are the same is that _____

_____

_____

_____ .

We can be friends because _____

_____

_____

_____ .

I think you are fun because _____

_____

_____

_____ .

Class Mural

This unit provides resources for you and your students to make an abstract mural together. Each person will contribute an individual picture to the abstract mural. The purpose of the mural is for students to learn more about themselves and each other. It also helps you to learn more about each of your students. As you introduce this project to students, keep in mind that some students may be happy to share details about themselves, while others may not feel comfortable doing so. It is important to create a safe space for students to share without feeling judged or uncomfortable about who they are and where they come from. This is intended to be an inclusive experience that creates positive relationships and fosters understanding of each other.

Getting Started

Reproduce and distribute the student pages for each student and allow them to complete the pages. Provide colored pencils, crayons, or markers for students for the activity pages, and provide the materials listed for the Creating the Class Mural pages (pages 142–144).

1. What Is a Mural? (page 133)

Distribute one copy of this page to each student. This activity is intended to introduce murals to students and to help students start thinking about murals. It also tells students that they will create a mural together as a class. Explain to students that they can use their mural picture to tell about themselves. Explain that they can also learn about their classmates from the class mural.

2. Shapes for Your Mural (page 134)

Distribute one copy of this page to each student. The purpose of this activity is to help students practice drawing shapes and to help them think about what shapes they might use. Explain to students that this page is for practice and that they do not have to use the shapes they draw on this page in their final project.

3. About Your Family (page 135)

Distribute one copy of this page to each student. This activity will guide students to think about their families and what they might want to include about their family in their mural picture. Explain to students that they may choose to make a picture that shows something about their family, but they do not have to.

4. About Yourself (page 136)

Distribute one copy of this page to each student. This activity will guide students to reflect about themselves and what they might want to share about themselves. Remind students that their pictures will show something that they want to share about their families or themselves.

5. **Colors for Your Mural (page 137)**

   Distribute one copy of this page to each student. This activity will help students think about what colors they want to use in their picture. Some students may have an idea of what they want to create, and they may choose colors based on their ideas so far (such as team or flag colors). Encourage students to be creative and think about the colors they might choose to use.

6. **Pictures for Your Mural (pages 138–139)**

   Distribute one copy of each page to each student. Explain to students that they may choose to cut out the pictures on these pages and glue or tape them to their mural. Explain that they can color these pictures with paint, markers, crayons, or colored pencils. Some students may need additional copies of the cut-out pictures.

7. **Stamps for Your Mural (page 140)**

   Distribute one copy of the page to each student. Provide students with colorful paints and objects to use as stamps.

8. **Patterns for Your Mural (page 141)**

   Distribute one copy of the page to each student. This activity may help students decide whether or not to use patterns in their mural picture.

9. **Creating the Class Mural (pages 142–144)**

   Sketch Your Mural Picture   (page 142)

   Distribute one copy of this page to each student. This page is intended to be the final draft page, which students can use to practice making their pictures. Explain to students that they can use this page to draw what their final picture will look like. Remind students to include shapes, colors, and pictures. Tell students that they can cut out pictures from pages 138 and 139 and put them on their draft if they choose to.

   Mural Picture Directions and Mural Picture Page   (pages 143 and 144)

   Provide students with the materials listed on page 143 below What You Need. Distribute one copy of pages 143 and 144 to each student. Guide students as they follow the steps below What You Do to make their individual pictures for the class mural.

   Putting the Pictures Together to Make the Class Mural

   Collect each student's picture. Then attach all of the pictures together using a stapler or tape, or using tacks on a bulletin board, corkboard, or tackboard. You may choose to have students help put the pictures together.

   After the individual pictures are put together, decide where to place the class abstract mural so that it can be seen.

   Encourage students to look at the pictures and use them to try to learn about their classmates.

Name _____

What Is a Mural?

You will make a mural with your classmates. A mural is a big picture, and it's usually on a wall. The picture or pictures in a mural have meaning. Your mural picture can tell about you or what you like. Look at the pictures of murals below. An **abstract mural** has lots of different pictures in it.

Mural on a library wall

Cpl. Jackeline Perez Rivera, Public domain, via Wikimedia Commons

Abstract mural that a group of people made

Name _____

Shapes for Your Mural

You will make a picture for your class mural. Think about shapes you might want to use in your mural picture. Answer the items below.

1. Look at the shapes in the row. Then in the rectangle, draw a picture made of only these shapes.

2. Draw a cloud shape.

3. Write 3 shapes you see in this mural.

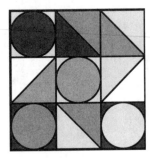

_____

_____

_____

Name _____

About Your Family

Think about your family. What do you do together? Do you have a pet?
What languages do you and your family speak with each other?
Answer the items below.

1. Write one thing that you would like to share about your family.
You can tell anything.

_____

_____

2. Draw a picture that
shows something you
like to do with your family.

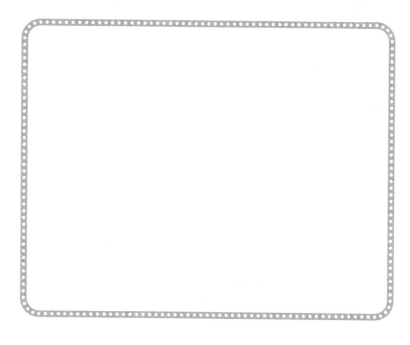

3. What country is your family from? You can write more than
one country.

_____

_____

4. Write a special food that you and your family like to make
or eat together.

_____

Name _____

About Yourself

Think about what you would like to tell other people about yourself.
What do you want people to know about you? Answer the items.

1. Draw or write something that
you like in the square.
For example, do you like...

2. Draw or write something that
you like to do or something
that you're good at.

3. Draw or write a place you
went to that you want to tell
other people about.

Culturally Responsive Lessons and Activities • EMC 8262 • © Evan-Moor Corporation

Name _____

Colors for Your Mural

Think about what you want to show in your mural picture. Think about the colors you will use. Answer the items.

1. Color the circles with some colors you might use in your picture.

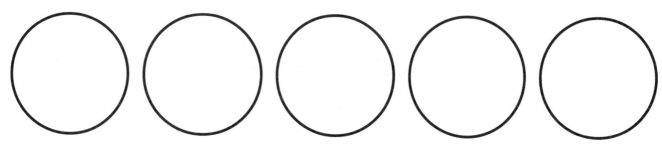

2. Is there a sports team that you and your family like? Color the stars the team's colors. Or color the stars any colors you like.

3. What is your favorite color? Write it.

_____

4. Color the crayon with your best friend's favorite color.

Name _____

Pictures for Your Mural

Look at the pictures below and on page 139. If you want to use any of the
pictures in your mural sketch or picture, cut them out and color them.

Culturally Responsive Lessons and Activities • EMC 8262 • © Evan-Moor Corporation

Name _____

Stamps for Your Mural

Use objects as stamps. Dip different objects in paint and press them onto the paper inside the square. See how the stamp pictures look. You might want to use them in your final mural picture.

These are objects you might choose to use as stamps:

orange slices   strawberry slices   cucumber slices   sponges

leaves   apple slices   cotton balls   flowers

Culturally Responsive Lessons and Activities • EMC 8262 • © Evan-Moor Corporation

Name _____

Patterns for Your Mural

Look at the patterns inside the rectangles. Copy each pattern by drawing it in the other rectangle.

1.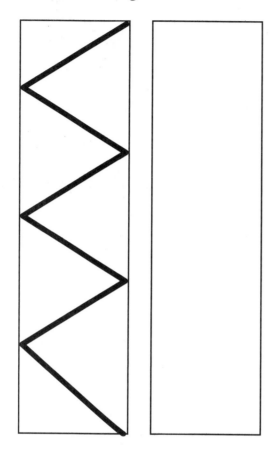

2.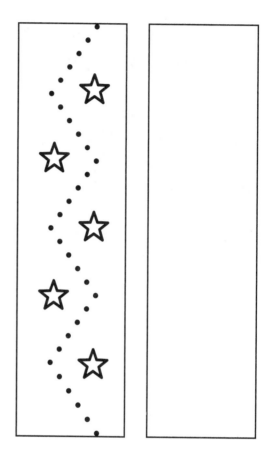

Look at the pattern. Draw shapes to copy the pattern under the line. Think about if you want to use patterns in your mural picture.

3.

Name _____

Sketch Your Mural Picture

Draw to show what your mural picture will look like. You can use words, letters, numbers, or other symbols, too.

1. Look at your answers from the other pages to get ideas of what to paint or draw.

2. You may choose to cut out and color the pictures on pages 138 and 139 to use below and in your final picture.

Remember, your mural picture can tell about your family or yourself.

Culturally Responsive Lessons and Activities • EMC 8262 • © Evan-Moor Corporation

Name_____

Mural Picture Directions

Make a mural picture to tell about your family or yourself. Your picture will be part of a big class mural.

What You Need

- pages 138, 139, and 144
- paintbrush and paint
- a sheet of construction paper
- scissors
- markers, crayons, or colored pencils
- glue or tape

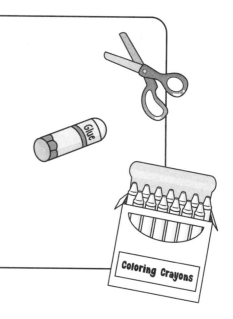

What You Do

1. On page 144, make your mural picture. Use a paintbrush and paint. Or you may choose to use markers, crayons, or colored pencils.

   If you choose to cut out pictures from pages 138 or 139, first color the pictures with paint, markers, crayons, or colored pencils. Next, cut out the pictures. Last, tape or glue the pictures onto page 144.

2. After you finish making your mural picture, cut on the dotted line to cut off the page title. Then glue or tape your mural picture onto the construction paper.

3. Give your mural picture to your teacher.